PRAISE FOR

RESTORING YOUR SHIELD OF FAITH

This well-written book brought me to a new level of faith and belief that I had not walked in previously. Reading these concepts is rather like eating spiritual Wheaties. For those of you who have had some serious challenges to your faith of late, *Restoring Your Shield of Faith* is for you!

CINDY JACOBS
AUTHOR, *THE VOICE OF GOD*

It's remarkable how Chuck Pierce and Robert Heidler always hit the bull's-eye. *Restoring Your Shield of Faith* imparts classic teaching about foundational principles, yet it unfolds these truths in a fresh and relevant way. We all need to hear this message. Both of these men have faced very tough spiritual battles and have learned firsthand how to lift high their shields of faith. Read their stories, soak in their teaching, and become better equipped to face the enemy and enter a new dimension of your walk with God.

DR. DUTCH SHEETS
AUTHOR, *INTERCESSORY PRAYER*

Restoring Your Shield of Faith challenges our lack of faith when trouble or adversity comes our way. Chuck Pierce and Robert Heidler carefully unfold a tapestry of biblical truths to help us act in faith to receive the promises of God. Read this book and your faith will ignite as mine did!

ALICE SMITH
EXECUTIVE DIRECTOR, U.S. PRAYER CENTER

Do you want to live God's full destiny for your life? It will only happen if you live a life of vibrant faith. *Restoring Your Shield of Faith* is a book that will help you begin a new journey and sustain the faith that you need to move forward.

C. PETER WAGNER
CHANCELLOR, WAGNER LEADERSHIP INSTITUTE

In today's world of chaos and confusion, Christians need a new level of faith. Many people have become discouraged, faced fears they never encountered before or lost hope. *Restoring Your Shield of Faith* gives a practical road map for regaining a powerful level of faith that secures the victory. I highly recommend this book to help anyone shift into a new place and obtain the promises of the Lord for their life.

BARBARA WENTROBLE
FOUNDER, INTERNATIONAL BREAKTHROUGH MINISTRIES
AUTHOR, *PROPHETIC INTERCESSION* AND *YOU ARE ANOINTED*

RESTORING YOUR
SHIELD
of
FAITH

CHUCK D. PIERCE
ROBERT HEIDLER

Regal

From Gospel Light
Ventura, California, U.S.A.

PUBLISHED BY REGAL BOOKS
FROM GOSPEL LIGHT
VENTURA, CALIFORNIA, U.S.A.
Regal PRINTED IN THE U.S.A.

Regal Books is a ministry of Gospel Light, an evangelical Christian publisher dedicated to serving the local church. We believe God's vision for Gospel Light is to provide church leaders with biblical, user-friendly materials that will help them evangelize, disciple and minister to children, youth and families.

It is our prayer that this Regal book will help you discover biblical truth for your own life and help you meet the needs of others. May God richly bless you.

For a free catalog of resources from Regal Books/Gospel Light, please call your Christian supplier or contact us at 1-800-4-GOSPEL *or* www.regalbooks.com.

Edited by Steven Lawson

Library of Congress Cataloging-in-Publication Data

Pierce, Chuck D., 1953–
    Restoring your shield of faith / Chuck D. Pierce and Robert Heidler.
        p. cm.
    Includes bibliographical references and index.
    ISBN 0-8307-3263-2
    1. Spiritual warfare. 2. Christian life. 3. Faith. I. Heidler,
Robert D., 1948– II. Title.
    BV4509.5.P55 2003
    235'.4–dc22   2003021385

1 2 3 4 5 6 7 8 9 10 11 12 13 14 15 / 09 08 07 06 05 04 03

Rights for publishing this book in other languages are contracted by Gospel Light Worldwide, the international nonprofit ministry of Gospel Light. Gospel Light Worldwide also provides publishing and technical assistance to international publishers dedicated to producing Sunday School and Vacation Bible School curricula and books in the languages of the world. For additional information, visit www.gospellightworldwide.org; write to Gospel Light Worldwide, P.O. Box 3875, Ventura, CA 93006; or send an e-mail to info@gospellightworldwide.org.

CONTENTS

*Put on the full armor of God, . . . with the
belt of truth buckled around your waist,
with the breastplate of righteousness in place,
and with your feet fitted with the readiness
that comes from the gospel of peace.*
In addition to all this, take up the shield of
faith, *with which you can extinguish all the
flaming arrows of the evil one.*

EPHESIANS 6:13-16, *NIV,*
EMPHASIS ADDED

THE TESTUDO

Through the early morning mist Severus Maximus could see barbarian warriors amassing at the far end of the valley. For six months these enemy combatants had been raiding wagons that traveled along Roman trade routes in the region. Severus and his cohort of 600 Roman soldiers had been dispatched to clear them out.

Severus's men knew their jobs well, but going into battle was never taken lightly. Tension filled the air as they quietly and efficiently donned their armor. The youngest of the cohort, Valentinus, visibly trembled as he adjusted the straps on his armor. Not yet out of his teens, he was about to taste battle for the first time.

When Severus approached, Valentinus snapped to attention.

Severus carefully checked the young man's armor and then ordered, "Pick up your equipment!"

The young recruit knelt and picked up his sword and his large rectangular shield. The battle shield held Severus's attention. It was Rome's secret weapon and the key to many battlefield victories. Amazingly light, it was nonetheless firm enough and large enough to give a soldier almost complete protection. A nervous Valentinus stood to attention, holding his shield closely by his side—it was almost as tall as he was.

"Young Valentinus, you are now a Roman soldier," Severus announced. "You are part of the best-trained, best-equipped fighting force the world has ever seen."

The commander put his hand on the young man's shoulder and softened his tone, "You were sent here to face this barbarian horde. But remember this, you were not sent here to die. You were sent here to win! Keep your shield up and you will do well."

As the young man's eyes brightened, Severus smiled slightly, "Strength and honor, Valentinus."

"Strength and honor, sir."

Across the valley the barbarian warlord was preparing his men for battle also. His camp was quite a contrast to the one Severus ran. It reeked of unwashed bodies and spoiled food. The men were poorly trained, ill equipped and shaggy in appearance. However, their stench and paint-streaked faces had struck terror into the hearts of many a foe.

The barbarian horde was divided into two groups. On the front lines were 700 warriors. Armed with swords, lances and axes, they milled about, laughing and boasting of their prowess. Each seemed eager to prove that he was stronger and louder than the others. The second flank consisted of 200 archers, their arrows tipped with black pitch, which would be deadly to their enemies.

The warlord was proud of his men. They had seen many battles and had always been victorious. But they had never fought the Romans.

The moment the sound of a trumpet echoed across the valley the barbarians saw the Romans forming long lines and ranks. Soon the air was filled with an ominous sound, like low-pitched thunder. It was the rumble of marching feet and Roman swords rhythmically slapping the edge of large rectangular shields.

The barbarian hordes were not intimidated. Eager to taste blood, they began to curse and taunt the approaching Romans. Finally the warlord gave the signal. The first wave of enemy warriors let out a battle cry, lifted their weapons high over their heads and sprinted across the narrowing strip of land that separated the two forces.

To the horror of the warlord, the Romans responded with a tactic that he had never before seen. As the first wave of barbarians approached, the Roman soldiers—marching shoulder to shoulder—linked their shields together to form an impenetrable wall. The barbarians found themselves rushing headlong toward a solid mass that was moving inexorably toward them.

When the enemies clashed, the barbarian weapons harmlessly clanked against the Roman shields. The warlord could not believe his eyes: His brave warriors were quickly impaled on Roman swords that were thrust through narrow slits between the shields.

The barbarian leader signaled a second wave of attack but saw this force meet the same fate: dashed against the moving fortress of the Roman army. A third wave was just as rapidly repulsed. A few Roman soldiers fell, but they were instantly replaced by others who moved up from the rear.

As the Roman wall of shields continued to advance on the barbarians, the warlord shrieked in anger and gave a signal to his archers. Pitch-tipped arrows were dipped in firepots. At the warlord's next signal, the air above the Roman forces was filled with a storm of flaming arrows.

But once again the Romans were prepared. While the frontline soldiers kept their shields closely linked, the soldiers behind them lifted their shields overhead, fitting them together in a formation the Romans called the *testudo* (tortoise). The Roman line had been transformed into a roofed stronghold! Their linked shields quickly extinguished the flaming arrows and allowed the soldiers to continue their advance.

The barbarian warlord had no formal education, but he was no fool. He knew his forces were defeated, so they quickly retreated. As the barbarians fled across the valley and out of sight, Severus knew that because of their shields, another battle had been won. Just as the final clouds of dust were settling, Severus caught sight of Valentinus. The young man, who had been so nervous before the battle began, now stood tall, proud and victorious. "Strength and honor, sir," the Roman soldier said to his commander.

"Strength and honor, Valentinus," Severus beamed to the child who, by trusting in the strength of his shield, on this day and in this battle had become a man.

SHIELD OF FAITH

Words and music by Ron Block
Recorded by Grammy Award-winner Alison Krauss

Sometimes I'm battle weary
I forget to use my shield
The arrows pierce my armor
And I stumble in the field

A shield won't do much good if it's hangin' by your side
Keep the shield of faith before you if you want to stay alive

I'll think my life is over
But the Lord he comes to me
He heals my wounded spirit
And he sets me on my feet

A shield won't do much good if it's hangin' by your side
Keep the shield of faith before you if you want to stay alive

Sometimes you're battle weary
But the war's already won
Keep your head and hold your shield high
'Til your days of life are done

A shield won't do much good if it's hangin' by your side
Keep the shield of faith before you if you want to stay alive
Keep the shield of faith before you if you want to stay alive

CHAPTER 1

JESUS, OUR SHIELD

When we become Christians, we are born onto a battle-field. Our choice is not whether we want to enter into a conflict; rather, war has already been declared against us. Our only choice is whether we want to be trampled by the enemy or learn to fight and win.

At issue in this battle are the promises of God. Peter said that God has given us His precious and magnificent assurances and that through them we can become partakers of His divine nature (see 2 Pet. 1:4). God has given us promises that relate to every area of life. He has promised us abundant provision, healing and many other blessings.

THE BATTLE BEGINS

God guarantees much to people who put their trust in Him. However, when we open our Bible and begin to claim these promises, we discover the battle! When we say "I want to come into a new place in the Lord! I want to move forward to obtain the promises!" Satan—our enemy in this battle—will try to stop us. Satan's goal is to frighten and discourage us, to cause us to turn back and not press on.

Often when we start moving forward, we also start seeing things go wrong in our lives. Sometimes Satan unleashes one great, overwhelming attack. For example, just when we begin to trust the Lord for our finances, an unexpected bill arrives in the mail. We open the envelope and almost faint! All of our faith washes down the drain. If it is not a bill, then it may be a prolonged illness or some other setback that impedes our progress.

Sometimes a storm of adversity comes upon us. We start to take huge steps forward and walk closer to the Lord than ever before, when suddenly we are barraged by calamities. We figure that the attack must be spiritual, because what has slammed into us is far beyond a normal run of bad luck! A friend of Robert Heidler described these storms of adversity this way: "You can always tell when it is Satan, because he always overplays his hand."[1]

Such attacks may affect our health. When John Dickson left his career in the secular world to become a full-time worship leader in the church I attend (Glory of Zion Outreach), it seemed as if the enemy resisted him on every side. The day he came on staff, two of his kids came down with chicken pox, one developed pinkeye and his wife got sick! His family was in such turmoil that for two weeks, taking care of them took up all of his time. Just when John's family began to recover, his own back went out. He was flat on his back and gone for another two weeks.

Sometimes a storm of adversity seems to blow hard on our finances. When pastor Robert Heidler began to shift Glory of Zion Outreach, a traditional Bible church, toward the new apostolic movement (emphasizing gifts and the biblical positions of authority, including apostles, prophets, etc.), adverse winds began to blow. We entered a phase when God was establishing some major new ministries through the church. In the midst of this crucial time, a wave of adversity crashed down upon Robert's family. First, their hot water heater sprang a leak and

SATAN COMES WITH A STORM OF ADVERSITY TO INTIMIDATE US AND TRY TO MAKE US TURN BACK.

the flood of water ruined their carpet. They had to get the carpet *and* the hot water heater replaced. As they were working to get these accomplished, the alternator on their car went out and termites invaded their house. Then the thermostat in their car malfunctioned, causing it to overheat. The fuel pump was next to go down, leaving Robert and his family stranded. In a three-week period this storm of adversity not only consumed much of their time and attention, but it also resulted in more than $3,000 in repair bills. Talk about distracting, hindering forces!

The Enemy Who Attacks
Most Christians who try to advance along the path to which God has called them have experienced spiritual attacks. Satan comes with a storm of adversity to intimidate us and try to make

us turn back. We will take a closer look at this in chapter 4, but let's become familiar with the diabolical schemes of the enemy from the start.

The apostle Paul described spiritual warfare in the book of Ephesians: "Take up the shield of faith, with which you can extinguish all the flaming arrows of the evil one" (6:16, *NIV*). The people of Ephesus experienced the greatest revival the Church in that day had seen. How did Paul get believers to a place of faith to experience this? As described in the book of Ephesians, first he prayed that they would have resting upon them what I call a spirit of wisdom and revelation. He then helped reveal each believer's identity in Christ. He encouraged them to be rooted and grounded in love. He admonished them to put off all idolatry and to put on Christ. "To put on Christ" means not only to raise Him up as a model but also to invite His Holy Spirit to live within and work through us. Paul made this clear to the Christians of his day.

The apostle also stressed the importance of the ascension, or government, (church leadership) gifts that would bring believers into a unity of faith. He then encouraged members of the Early Church to get all of their earthly affairs in order. He revealed that understanding proper alignment and authority was extremely important. There was a clear order and progression in what Paul taught. After laying out the initial steps, the apostle said, "Therefore put on the full armor of God" (Eph. 6:13, *NIV*). It was the shield that would quench every flaming arrow that would come against them—likewise, it is the shield that will protect us.

Roman Shields That Protect

As Paul saw the kind of attack Satan unleashed against God's people, he perceived that the spiritual warfare of Christians is analogous to the physical warfare of the Roman army.

As illustrated in the prologue of this book, in ancient warfare it was common for armies to use a storm of arrows to terrify their enemies. If we were soldiers and thousands of flaming arrows began to strike all around us, the number one thing in our mind would be, *I've got to get out of here!* Sometimes that is how we feel when Satan attacks us.

The Roman army had a piece of armor that provided a solid defense against this kind of attack. In many cases it was the secret weapon that brought the army victory. This piece of armor was the battle shield.

As I described in the prologue, this shield was not like the round metal discs we often see in movies. The Roman battle shield was a large rectangular defense of metal that covered the entire length of a man's body. Roman soldiers would line up shoulder to shoulder with their shields held in front of them and move across the battlefield like an armored tank. When the apostle Paul thought about our struggle against Satan, he realized that God has given us a shield like that. It is a shield of faith.

When Paul described our shield, he used the word for the Roman battle shield. The word is *thureos,* and it means a door-shaped shield (the Greek word for door is *thura*).[2]

The thureos was a large rectangular shield about five feet high and three feet wide. It was also called a castle shield. In other words, it was a portable fortress. I found it interesting to study how this shield was made. The thureos was very large; therefore, if it had been made of solid wood or metal, it would have been difficult to carry. To construct a thureos the Romans began with a wooden framework. Over that framework they fastened seven layers of tough leather from the skin of a bull or a calf, until the shield was four or five inches thick, and then nailed them securely in place. As the soldiers got ready to go into battle, they dipped the shield in a nearby river to saturate it with water so it would not only stop an arrow, but it would also quench the fire.[3]

Our Shield Who Is Named Jesus

As I studied the Roman shield, God began to give me a revelation. Just think about how this shield was constructed. The skin of a bull or calf was stretched out over a wooden frame. In the Old Testament, the animal required for a sin offering was a bull or a calf. The skin of the bull or calf is a symbol of a *sacrifice* for sin.

A single layer of leather was not sufficient for the Roman shield to be effective. The shield maker built up seven layers of animal skin to provide the necessary protection. Seven is the number of perfection. This provides a picture of a *perfect* sacrifice. The perfect sacrifice was stretched out and nailed to a wooden framework. Its purpose was to take upon itself all of the arrows intended for the soldier.

GOD HAS GIVEN US A SHIELD AND HIS NAME IS JESUS!

Look at what this shield represents. God has provided a perfect sacrifice for sin through His Son, Jesus. This perfect sacrifice was stretched out and nailed to a wooden cross. *His purpose was to receive upon Himself all the afflictions Satan intended for us!*

God wants us to know that *He has given us a shield* and *His name is Jesus!* Jesus came to be our shield. He came to take upon Himself every arrow that Satan intended for us.

- *Jesus took our guilt.* God caused the guilt of us all to fall on His Son (see Isa. 53:6). Jesus took our guilt so that we can have His righteousness.
- *He took our infirmities.* He bore our sicknesses and our weaknesses upon Himself so that we can be healed (see Isa. 53:4-5).
- *He took our poverty.* "Though he was rich, yet for your sakes he became poor, so that you through his poverty might become rich" (2 Cor. 8:9, *NIV*). Jesus took our poverty so that we can have His abundance.
- *He took our curse.* He became a curse for us, so that the blessing of Abraham would come on the Gentiles by faith (see Gal. 3:13-14). Jesus took the curse so that we can have the blessing.

When Jesus hung on the cross, He interposed Himself between us and our enemy. It was His will that all the evil Satan intends for us would come upon Him instead.

We need to realize that when an arrow of the enemy strikes us, it is a violation of the will of God. Jesus wants those arrows to come on *Him*, so we do not have to bear them. Jesus came to be our shield, but we don't experience His protection unless we activate our shield by faith. In fact, this is true of everything Jesus did for us—without faith we cannot experience deliverance, restoration or anything else He wants for us.

This is true of salvation. Think about this: How many people in the world did Jesus die for?

All of them.

How many people in the world already have salvation purchased for them?

Everybody!

If someone exists for whom Jesus has not *already* purchased salvation, He would need to die again in order for that person to be saved. He's not going to do that because He does not need to. When Jesus went to the cross, He paid it all, for everyone. He has already purchased salvation for every person who has ever been born and everyone who ever will be born.

There is a catch, however. Only those who exercise *faith* will actually obtain and experience what He has already purchased for them. In the same way, Jesus purchased protection for every believer. He hung on the cross as our shield to take all the arrows of the enemy upon Himself.

But only when we have faith is our shield activated. To put it another way, only when we have faith do we experience the protection Jesus has already purchased for us.

The remainder of this book is predicated on the assumption that we are believers in Christ, for without taking that first step of faith, we can never raise our shield of faith.

OUR SHIELD GOES UP

How do we activate our shield of faith?

We trigger it by standing on God's Word. As believers, we naturally should seek to do this in every area of life. As we learn to do this, we will see that when the battles come, we are ready. For example, we might come under attack financially. The flaming arrows of the enemy fall on every side. We become overwhelmed by our need. How do we lift up our shield and come under God's protection?

Promises That God Keeps

The first step: We need to know what God has promised. Too many Christians don't know God's promises. Some have been told it is

God's will for us to live in poverty. If we believe that lack of provision is what God wants, then we will never have faith to overcome a financial setback. In fact, we will probably become irresponsible, which will make the problem worse rather than improve it.

We need to know God's will. Where do we find God's will? It is revealed in the Bible. To bolster our trust in God for our finances, we can read passages that describe God's will for us to prosper.

Psalm 23:1 is one of those verses. It reads, "The LORD is my shepherd; I shall not want." This verse is very clear. God says His standard is that we be short of nothing that we need.

Everybody loves to recite Psalm 23. We sing about it, talk about it, utter it at funerals and put it on wall plaques. Psalm 23 makes us feel good when we read it, but there is not one Christian in a hundred who believes this promise is true—by "believe" I mean applying it in our life and expecting it to happen.

A lot of Christians claim to believe the Bible but make silly comments such as "I don't believe in that prosperity stuff." What happened to Psalm 23? If God's Word says the Lord is our

BECAUSE JESUS IS OUR SUN AND SHIELD, HE WILL NOT WITHHOLD ANY GOOD THING FROM US.

shepherd, then He is our shepherd and we will have no lack.

Let's look at two other passages.

Psalm 34:9 (NIV) promises us, "Those who fear him lack nothing."

Psalm 84:11 (NIV) expands upon the promise: "The LORD God is a sun and shield; . . . no good thing does he withhold from those whose walk is blameless." God wants us to know that He is our sun (our provider) and our shield (our protector). Because He is our sun and shield, He will not withhold any good thing from us.

That's the promise of God's Word. If we walk with God and adhere to His standard, then His will for our lives is that we lack no good thing. Having enough is supposed to be the norm, not the miraculous exception.

Yet many Christians live continually in poverty and need.

Why is this?

There are many reasons, but in too many cases it's because we are willing to live in poverty.

What do we do when the mailman comes to our door to deliver a package and we realize that he has delivered it to the wrong address?

We say, "I can't take that. It's not mine."

Yet when Satan comes to our door to deliver poverty to us, what do we tend to say?

"Oh yes, thank you. I'll take that!"

That is not the right answer. Jesus wants us to look the devil in the eye and say, "This poverty isn't mine! Jesus took my poverty! You're delivering this to the wrong person!"

The Word declares, "You know the grace of our Lord Jesus Christ, that though he was rich, yet for your sakes he became poor, so that you through his poverty might become rich" (2 Cor. 8:9, *NIV*).

A Mistake That Promotes Poverty

In the fourth century, the Church made one of the biggest mistakes in history. Under the influence of the Roman emperor Constantine, the Church bought into Greek philosophy and paganism. Part of what Christians of that day allowed themselves to get mixed up with was the idea that everything material is evil and everything spiritual is good. That is not biblical.

The Church accepted the pagan idea that if we want to be holy, we have to renounce everything material. In that day, one of the three vows men who wanted to serve God were required to take was a vow of poverty (the other two were obedience and chastity).

The Church began to teach that Jesus set an example of poverty for us to follow. The reasoning went like this: Jesus was holy and He lived in poverty, so if we want to be holy, we should live in poverty also.

That is not what the Bible teaches! The Bible shows us that He became poor, so that we might become rich.

Jesus did not suffer poverty to be our example. Jesus suffered poverty to be our deliverer. He took our poverty upon Himself so that we can avoid it. The Bible teaches in no uncertain terms that poverty is a curse, and the Father does not want His children walking under a curse.

There is a lot of crazy thinking in the Church about this! Let me make this clear. Poverty does not make us holy. Most of the holy men in the Bible were not poor. Abraham was rich. Apart from one brief period of adversity, Job lived his life in incredible abundance. David was a king who enjoyed tremendous wealth. Paul had tremendous success as a church planter. He started many churches and saw many of them grow to thousands of members. All along he boasted that he had all of the supplies he needed.

Is prosperity demanding that God give us a stock-market windfall, a house in Maui or a Lexus SUV? No. God may grant us one or all of these items, but the endless accumulation of possessions just for the sake of accumulating possessions is not what the Bible promises. If we only go for the gold, then material gain will command our attention and eventually displace Jesus as our god. When we walk in faith, our focus must be on

Jesus, not on specific riches. Read the verses again. They promise that when we walk in faith, we will lack nothing. That means we should not be living in poverty.

Verses That Unveil the Curse

Poverty is a curse. We can find the details in the Old Testament. Deuteronomy 28:1-14 describes the blessings of God. God's blessings include things such as success, prosperity and God's blessing the work of our hands.

In Deuteronomy 28:15-46 we read a description of the curses. The curses include sickness, infirmity, oppression and poverty. Deuteronomy 28:48 sums up the curse of poverty as being hunger, thirst, nakedness, lack of everything good, and oppression by our enemies. That is total and complete poverty!

Remember, we are using financial setbacks as an example of when and how to raise our shields of faith. The first step is to know the promise of God in that area. Now we have a better understanding of what God desires and we are ready to lift the shield.

A Response That Defeats Our Enemy

When an unexpected bill comes in the mail, when everything in the house breaks at once, when we have medical expenses our insurance will not cover, Satan can twist it all into a financial catastrophe. We cannot let that happen. We must raise our shield of faith and break the power of hunger, thirst, nakedness, lack of everything good, and oppression by our enemy. These conditions of poverty do not make us holy. When they knock at our door, we must move from the curse into God's blessing.

Remember that when Jesus hung on the cross, He fully bore the poverty curse for us. Years ago I heard Bible teacher Derek Prince give a message on this. He pointed out that when Jesus was crucified, He was hungry! He hadn't eaten for 24 hours.

Some of His last words from the cross were "I thirst!" (John 19:28). And Jesus hung on the cross absolutely naked! They had taken from Him everything He owned. He suffered lack of everything and was taunted and oppressed by His enemies. The totality of the poverty curse came and rested upon Him. He took on Himself the curse that was intended for us.

Jesus hung on the cross as our shield! He took our poverty so that we can have His provision. Because Jesus took our poverty, we can claim His promise, "My God will meet all of your needs according to his glorious riches in Christ Jesus" (Phil. 4:19, *NIV*). The price has been paid, but we must activate our shield of faith. Just as there will be people who go to hell, even though Jesus purchased their forgiveness, so there are Christians who live in poverty, even though Jesus purchased their provision.

OUR FAITH WORKS

In this book we will learn how to begin walking with our shield of faith in place. I encourage you to begin by making some declarations of faith.

1. Identify the arrows Satan is sending to keep you from advancing. Ask yourself, *What things has Satan placed in my life to keep me from moving forward in the Lord?* Know that these attacks are designed to keep you from growing in the Lord and from fulfilling your destiny. By faith, thank God that Jesus took upon Himself *all* of the evil Satan intended for you.

2. By faith, declare God's blessing as your portion. Come into agreement with God that because He is your shepherd, you shall not lack anything He has intended for you. Declare that He took your sickness

and infirmity so that you could walk in health. Praise Him that He took upon Himself the curse so that you can inherit the blessing. Thank Him that He does not want you to live as a mere man or woman but as a person empowered by God.

3. By faith, choose to reject discouragement and fear. Ask God to begin to reveal His strategy to overcome whatever Satan will bring to your front door. Thank Him that He has a way for you to break through.

4. Finally, by faith, set your eyes on the goal and begin to move forward. Don't be hindered by the arrows. Set your heart in position to move forward. Know that you have a big shield. Take hold of it with both hands and hold it up in confidence. Find your place in God's army and stand shoulder to shoulder with others who are moving forward in the Lord.

Take your stand in faith! Declare victory! Declare that the Body of Christ is moving forward! Declare that every arrow is being quenched! Thank the Lord Jesus Christ for hanging on the cross for you. The cross has become a door for you. It has opened the way for your eternal destiny. Thank Him that His death on the cross has formed a shield on your behalf.

Notes

1. Pat Jarrard, personal communication to Robert Heidler, 1983.
2. James Strong, *The New Strong's Exhaustive Concordance of the Bible* (Nashville, TN: Thomas Nelson Publishers, 1984), ref. nos. 2375 (thureos) and 2374 (thura).
3. Kathleen Parker, "Spiritual Warfare: Strategies for Spiritual Battles," *Spiritual Survival*, 1999-2003. http://www.spiritualsurvival.org/view/?pageID=756 (accessed September 29, 2003).

CHAPTER 2

WHAT FAITH IS

Peter says our faith is more precious than gold (see 1 Pet. 1:7). In fact, faith is the central concept of Christianity. We can be called Christians only if we have faith. Therefore, if we are going to be able to understand what our shield of faith is and how to raise it, then we must better understand faith itself.

THE IMPORTANCE OF FAITH

Faith is related to every part of our Christian lives. *By faith* we receive salvation (see Eph. 2:8-9). Our experiences of sanctification (see Acts 26:18), purification (see Acts 15:9), justification (see Rom. 4:5; 5:1) and adoption (see Gal. 3:26; Col. 3:24) are all dependent upon our faith.

Faith was one of the main thrusts of Jesus' ministry. In the Gospels, we continually find statements such as "Your *faith* has healed you." In Jesus' hometown, He could not do mighty miracles because the people there lacked faith. He wasn't powerless to do so, but the atmosphere in that place prevented our Lord from exhibiting the power of faith. However, whenever He found men and women of faith, He released His power, and miracles took place. God assures us that *if we believe,* then nothing is impossible, and He withholds nothing.

The Bible teaches that if we can *get in* faith and *stay in* faith, everything else will come (see Matt. 8:13; 15:28; Mark 9:23). I don't care what needs we face in our life, if we can move into a position of faith and stay there, we will walk in victory on a day-to-day basis.

The Greek word for faith is *pistis.* It means to have trust or confidence. When we walk in faith, we are trusting and showing confidence in God in the midst of our situation. Jesus' call to "have faith in God" (Mark 11:22) was an exhortation to enter into a trusting commitment to the Father in the midst of whatever we might face. When Jesus said, "Your faith has made you whole," He was teaching that *confidence in* or *allegiance to* God releases God's wholeness into our lives.

FAITH IS THE DYNAMIC INTERACTION OF OUR SPIRIT MAN WITH GOD.

Faith is not static. It is the dynamic interaction of our spirit man with God. We have each been given a measure of faith through the hearing of the Word (see Rom. 10:17). As we walk with the Lord, we are exhorted to increase our faith through living our faith (see Rom. 1:17). God wants us to put on faith (see 1 Thess. 5:8), to grow in faith (see 2 Cor. 10:15) and to have a steadfast faith (see 1 Cor. 15:58) that becomes a strong faith (see Rom. 4:19-20).

Faith is a fruit of the Holy Spirit (see Gal. 5:22). There is also a spiritual gift of faith (see 1 Cor. 12:8-9). In times of need, the Holy Spirit can release to us a greater measure of faith. However, unless our shield of faith is in place, we cannot see all of these dimensions of faith activated.

Now faith is the assurance (the confirmation, the title deed) of the things [we] hope for, being the proof of things [we] do not see and the conviction of their reality [faith perceiving as real fact what is not revealed to the senses] (Heb. 11:1, *AMP*).

What an incredible statement! In the midst of today's tumultuous world, faith becomes the most important issue. It is vital that we understand this aspect of our spiritual lives, yet there is so much confusion over it. Verse 2 of Hebrews 11, which is often called the faith chapter, holds a key: "For by [faith] the elders obtained a good testimony." These saints obtained a good reputation because they actively expressed their relationship with a holy God. Their personal holiness is not what they are known for in history; they are known because they trusted in, relied on and interacted with the God of the universe.

The elders *used* their faith. We must grasp this concept if we are to raise our shield of faith. We must know the same God that these witnesses knew. We cannot have an effective faith without understanding the dedication and relationship that those who have gone before us displayed. They show us how we can be victorious in the midst of, and in spite of, the circumstances that surround us.

The Lord is the most trustworthy person we will ever meet. For our faith to have substance, or realization, we must have a relationship with Him. The word "substance" means "to stand under."[1] James 4:7 reads, "Therefore, submit to God. Resist the devil and he will flee from you." The word "submission" also means to stand under. Therefore, for our faith to be realized in a tumultuous world, we must be fully submitted in relationship to God. R. T. Kendall gives wonderful insight into this aspect of faith:

> Faith is that which keeps us looking beyond what we can see with our natural senses, with such confidence that we know we shall not be disappointed. Faith looks beyond oneself, never within oneself. Faith always leads us outside ourselves. Why? Because faith perceives its object—God. The main insight the writer's statement conveys, however, is what faith is *not*. It is the "evidence of things not seen." The Greek is *pragmaton elegchos ou blepomenon*—literally, "persuasion of the works not seen." One is convinced that one will see them; one is truly persuaded that one will see them. But one does not see them at the moment. Therefore, faith is not *seeing* the tangible. If one sees now what one previously had been waiting for, it ceases to be called faith. Until what someone was waiting for literally appears, such waiting is graced with the title *faith*.[2]

THE OPPOSITE OF FAITH

There are many words that convey the idea of faith. Once we understand these words, we also get a glimpse of what faith is not. Here are 10 sets of words. The first word is equated with faith, the second is its opposite.

1. Trust—Mistrust

To have faith is to trust God and believe that He is, that He can be in us and that He also has promises just for us. The opposite of faith is mistrust. Psalm 37:3 declares, "Trust in the LORD, and do good." Proverbs 3:5 adds: "Trust in the LORD with all your heart."

To trust someone is to make them a refuge. Think of a baby bird that hides itself under its parent's feathers. David beautifully describes this concept in Psalm 57:1: "And in the shadow of Your wings I will make my refuge." If our life is characterized by mistrust, then we are not walking in faith. The enemy does not want us to walk in faith; therefore, he will do everything he can to break down and destroy reliable relationships in our life.

2. Belief—Unbelief

Faith is believing what God has said. Unbelief is the enemy of faith. When Satan plants unbelief in our mind and we choose to agree with it, we have quenched our faith. Hebrews 3:12 warns, "Beware, brethren, lest there be in any of you an evil heart of unbelief." Unbelief simply wants us to believe that God is not able. It creates an atmosphere that negates God's ability. When we fall for this line of thinking, we are unable to enter into the promises and plans God has for us. The real strategy of the enemy is to build a belief system within each of us that is contrary to who God is.

3. Loyalty—Betrayal

Faith is loyalty. Faith is standing with God in the place He has asked us to stand, no matter what the circumstances may be. Faith's opposite is betrayal. When we make a commitment of loyalty to God, we call it a covenant. Walking in loyalty is a sign that we are walking by faith. Walking in loyalty is a sign of covenant. Covenant signifies relationship.

It is difficult to overcome an act of betrayal. One of the greatest contrasts in the New Testament is between Jesus' loyalty and Judas's betrayal (see Luke 22). The act of betrayal wounds and becomes imbedded in our emotions. The result is that after a hurtful experience we then guard ourselves in our relationships.

WALKING IN LOYALTY IS A SIGN THAT WE ARE WALKING BY FAITH.

4. Fidelity—Unfaithfulness

Faith is fidelity. Fidelity is a faithful devotion to duty, obligations or vows. Unfaithfulness is a lack of faith. The faithfulness of God is the basis for our faith. To choose a path of unfaithfulness negates our ability to trust. God is faithful, and His faithfulness is not dependent upon our faith. However, our faith reflects His faithfulness.

5. Dependence—Independence

Faith is dependence. To depend on others means that we rely upon them and we are influenced by them. It usually means that who we are has, in part, been determined by something in the character of those people upon whom we depend. Dependence is also linked to submission. If we are dependent, then we rely upon someone else for existence, support and success. Proverbs 3:6 leaves no doubt about what we should do: "In all your ways acknowledge Him, and He shall direct your paths." In other words, when we depend upon God, He will straighten our paths.

An independent spirit that cannot trust in or submit to authority will not be able to walk in faith. When Jesus saw the centurion's understanding of authority in action, He said, "You have great faith!" (see Matt. 8:9-10).

6. Confidence—Insecurity

Faith is confidence. First John 5:14 (*AMP*) explains:

> And this is the confidence (the assurance, the privilege of boldness) which we have in Him: [we are sure] that if we ask anything (make any request) according to His will (in agreement with His own plan), He listens to and hears us.

The definition of the Greek word *peitho* is "confidence." This means to be convinced, to have an inward certainty, to win over, to prevail upon, to persuade, to induce a change of mind by the use of argument. The opposite of confidence is insecurity. If we are plagued by insecurity, we are agreeing with the voice of unbelief. Insecurity—which can also manifest itself as fear—is believing that God's promises will fail. Where there is true faith there is no room for insecurity or fear. I like what Phil Pringle wrote in his book *Faith*:

> Faith is a feeling of absolute confidence. It is David—running, laughing, to meet the giant. He is fully assured that God is with him. He is not trying to believe, or pretending to be bold, hoping that God is with him; neither is he confessing the word to himself hopefully to build his faith. No. He is full of confidence. He feels great. This man is dangerous! David knew beyond a

shadow of a doubt that he was looking at a "dead giant." Victory was his. Goliath's head was nailed to the wall. This made him feel fantastic. Faith makes you feel fantastic. David made history that day. He showed us that faith, with feeling, surely works! Faith is an attitude you have within you.[3]

7. Obedience—Disobedience

Faith is obedience. Throughout the Word of God faith is demonstrated through obedience. First John 3:24 reads, "Now he who keeps His commandments abides in Him, and He in him." I love what Mary, the mother of Jesus, was quoted as saying: "Whatever He says to you, do it" (John 2:5). This boils down

IF WE LOVE AND TRUST GOD, WE WILL DO WHAT HE ASKS US TO DO.

the whole issue of faith to a single sentence. If we love and trust God, we will do what He asks us to do. Disobedience reveals a lack of faith. When we disobey God, we are saying that we do not have faith that He knows best or that He can keep His promises. God has made it clear that we are to go into battle and He will protect us. If we say no, then we are not only disobeying Him, but we are also declaring that we do not have enough faith to believe that He will protect us.

8. Wholeness—Fragmentation

Faith is wholeness. When we are linked to God through faith, we can walk in peace and be whole. The enemy loves to fragment us, which is the opposite of wholeness. When we walk in peace, we have harmony, we are calm, and we trust in God. Any place in our life in which we don't have peace usually is a place that the enemy has broken to pieces. Where faith is absent there is fragmentation.

9. Witness—Silence

First John 5:11 (*AMP*) reads, "And this is that testimony (that evidence): God gave us eternal life, and this life is in His Son." To be saved we must confess our faith. We do this when we first believe, but that confession of faith should not be limited to a single moment in time. It should be an ongoing part of our life. That's what made the great cloud of witnesses (see Heb. 12:1) who they were—they confessed their faith no matter what the circumstances. In the midst of discouragement, they uttered their faith.

For our faith to be truly faith, we must be willing to speak up. The opposite of being a true witness for God is keeping silent. Silence, at times, can simply be unbelief and timidity. A believer is a witness. First John 5:10 summarizes this:

He who believes in the Son of God has the witness in himself; he who does not believe God has made Him a liar, because he has not believed the testimony that God has given of His Son.

If we move in faith, we will be bold witnesses—we will speak up.

10. Love—Hate

Faith is love. Second Thessalonians 3:5 reads, "Now may the Lord direct your hearts into the love of God and into the patience of

Christ." Galatians 5:6 adds to this point: "For in Christ Jesus nei-
ther circumcision nor uncircumcision avails anything, but faith
working through love."

We are accepted on the grounds of faith, not by any law or
rule. As we show love, our faith increases. Our faith becomes
energized when we allow ourselves to love God and people.
When we love one another, God abides in us.

Love has so many wonderful benefits. Love casts out fear.
Because we love God, we eagerly obey Him. Because we love
God, we easily show loyalty. Because we love God, we are able to
trust Him.

The opposite of love is hate. A person who says he is in the
light yet hates his brother is actually in darkness (see 1 John 2:9).
This means that if we walk in darkness, we will lose sight of
where we are going and the One whom we are following. Hatred
causes our faith to stop functioning.

A BAROMETER OF FAITH

Faith, as I have noted, is the foundation of our Christian life. If
we are going to restore and raise our shield of faith, then we
must understand what faith means and how intregal it is to our
connection with God. Basically, without faith we cannot please
Him, because we have no relationship with Him. With faith, all
is possible.

Before we move forward to the next chapter, take a
moment to measure your faith against the Scriptures and
compare your faith with the 10 sets of opposites. Where do you
stand? Do you need to take that first step of faith and commit
your life to Christ? You can do it now. Do you need to ask forgiveness for a lack of faith in any area of your relationship with

God? Do it before we proceed. Then you will be ready to take up your shield of faith.

Notes

1. *Merriam-Webster's Collegiate Dictionary*, 10th ed., s.v. "substance."
2. R. T. Kendall, *Believing God* (Charlotte, NC: MorningStar Publications, 1997), p. 13.
3. Phil Pringle, *Faith* (Dee Why, Australia: Pax Ministries, Pty Ltd, 2003), pp. 23-24.

CHAPTER 3

BLESSINGS
AND BENEFITS

God made a big promise to Abraham:

> Get out of your country, from your kindred and
> from your father's house, to a land that I will show
> you. I will make you a great nation; I will bless you
> and make your name great; and you shall be a
> blessing. I will bless those who bless you, and I will
> curse him who curses you; and in you all the fam-
> ilies of the earth shall be blessed (Gen. 12:1-3).

This promise from God was contingent upon
Abraham's leaving and following—not just for a short
time, but until he found the land that God would show

him. The promise also included mission, prosperity and blessing. Let's take a closer look.

THE BLESSINGS OF FAITH

In essence, God told Abraham, "If you will leave your idolatrous form of worship and follow Me, I will prosper you and align Myself with you so that you will be the prototype and many people will follow your example in the future."

In Romans, Paul describes how Abraham's demonstration of faith and his choice to follow God resulted in his justification. "Abraham believed God, and it was accounted to him for righteousness" (Rom. 4:3) The Greek word *logidzomai* means "accounted." To better understand this concept, think of a bowl. If we continuously pour water into the bowl, it will soon fill up and spill over. Another analogy would be a reconciled balance sheet. Romans 4:20 goes on to indicate that Abraham did not waiver in unbelief when God made His promise; rather, Abraham was strengthened through faith and gave glory to God. He was fully convinced that with God's help he was able to perform what he was promised. Romans 4:22 reinforces the point: "It was accounted to him for righteousness."

Abraham patiently awaited the fulfillment of what would seem to others an unfulfillable promise. Abraham's faith, however, was strengthened as he walked with and glorified God each day. He believed, and so have generations of people who have been inspired by his example.

R. T. Kendall expands on this point:

The heroes of Hebrews 11 are people who believed God. They are the writer's example to show that faith itself is not a New Testament innovation. Faith goes way back in time, claims the writer of Hebrews. There is nothing new about it at all. God hides His face in order that we might believe. He withholds the evidence of things visible that we might be persuaded by His Word alone! Faith, then, is the long parenthesis between the undeniable appearances of God's glory. When God appears, faith is no longer necessary. There are actually times when faith is eclipsed by such a sense of the majesty and glory of God that one is temporarily without the need of faith. These times are mountaintop experiences, such as when our Lord was transfigured before His disciples (see Matt. 17:1-9).[1]

 ANYONE WHO ENTERS INTO THE SAME FAITH THAT ABRAHAM EXHIBITED CAN BE GRAFTED INTO THE SAME BLESSINGS HE RECEIVED.

Anyone who enters into the same faith that Abraham exhibited can be grafted into the same blessings he received. Romans 11:23 explains: "And they also, if they do not continue in unbelief, will be grafted in, for God is able to graft them in again." When, by faith, we accept Christ as our personal Savior, we receive great blessings and benefits.

Hearing the Word
Romans 10:17 shows us how to take our first steps in faith: "So then faith comes by hearing, and hearing by the word of God." This has been a significant Scripture in my life. My wife, Pam,

and I were in a wonderful denominational church in the 1970s, a time when God was doing so much to revitalize and change us so that we could enter into all He had for us in the future. Every Sunday our pastor, Billy Crosby, would begin the service by saying, "I believe the Bible is the Word of God." He would then quote Hebrews 4:12:

> The word of God is living and powerful, and sharper than any two-edged sword, piercing even to the division of soul and spirit, and of joints and marrow, and is a discerner of the thoughts and intents of the heart.

Then our pastor would read Romans 10:17: "Faith comes by hearing, and hearing by the word of God." He would contend that if faith comes by hearing, and hearing by the Word of God, then the faith that the lost need in order to be saved comes from the hearing of the Word of God. He would also say that for those who have already been saved, faith to come into spiritual maturity also comes by hearing the Word of God.

Imagine hearing this message every Sunday. We listened closely until the words became our reality. This understanding of the Word of God is what formed my life and my belief system. By the confession of my mouth, it became what I believed.

Listing the Elements

Romans 10:17 declares, "So then faith comes." What does this mean? If we already have faith, how can faith come? When we read the entire chapter of Romans 10, we discover that faith includes confession. Therefore, it is necessary to confess that we have committed ourselves to serve God. Faith has a messenger: Usually, somebody speaks, we hear, and then faith explodes. Faith has a voice: It is perceptible. If I am listening to someone speak, I can detect his or her faith. Faith has a report: If we live by faith, then we will have a good reputation. Faith has a response: Once we hear and begin to speak forth what we've heard, then we respond by doing that which has produced faith within us. Therefore, faith is not a passive concept; it becomes very active in our expression.

We need to know—to be certain—that the voice of faith is trustworthy. Author Trevor Newport explains:

> If someone that you trust says something to you, then you will usually believe them because they are reliable. This is how faith works in simple terms. If someone says to you that they will meet you at a certain place and time, then you will *act on their word* and meet them. You have put your faith in that person's word. You heard a piece of information and acted on it. That is what faith is. God has made statements in His precious Word that He expects us to act upon and see results. As you read and understand His Word, then you need to act on what He says. James 1:22 says, "But be ye doers of the word and not hearers only, deceiving your own selves."[2]

We know that God is reliable and His Word is dependable. Therefore, if someone is walking in faith and living by the Word, then we can come to trust that person's voice, too. We turn to that person, not on the same level as God or the Bible, but because God chooses to work and speak through people.

Developing Discipline
Spiritual discipline is required for faith to be maintained. In the book *Possessing Your Inheritance,* Rebecca Sytsema and I outlined eight spiritual disciplines we need if we are to become faithful in

this tumultuous world. The disciplines include meditation, prayer, fasting, warfare, giving, work, worship and rest.[3] A description of the eight distinguishing characteristics of men and women of great faith is found in *Heroic Faith: How to Live a Life of Extreme Devotion*:

> What distinguishes heroic faith from the plain vanilla kind? What qualities mark the lives of those you long to be like? In looking closely at hundreds of Christian martyrs and other persecuted believers, we found several distinguishing characteristics. If you were to conduct your own survey, you would find these same eight qualities.

> 1. *They are energized by an eternal perspective.* Individuals with heroic faith see beyond this world to the eternal realities. Rather than live for the moment and for this world, they look to the next, knowing that this life is not all there is.
> 2. *They have an uncanny dependence on God.* This quality is evidenced primarily by a life bracketed by prayer. Those whose faith is of a heroic caliber talk to God as if they know Him, because they do. And because they believe He hears them, they are less anxious than most.
> 3. *They love the Word of God.* They love to read it, study it and hear it read as well as preached. Not every person with a dog-eared Bible is a hero of faith, but it is likely that all who are have well-worn copies of the Scriptures.

4. *They are outrageously courageous.* When it comes to standing up for what they believe in, they aren't inclined to sit on their hands. These people possess a heroic boldness that flows out of their perspective of, total dependence on, and love for God's Word.

5. *They are living examples of what it means to endure.* Quitting is not a concept with which they are familiar. And because faith heroes view life as a long-distance race, speed is not nearly as important as stamina.

6. *They take obedience very seriously.* Pleasing God matters much more than accommodating people's unpredictable expectations. Heroic disciples delight in doing what they know God desires.

7. *They are unquestionably self-controlled.* Men and women who serve as heroic examples to the rest of us are not victims as much as they are victorious. They decide what the circumstances call for and act accordingly, even if it means voluntarily laying down their lives.

8. *They are marked quite simply by love.* Their eyes do not lie. Their countenance can warm the coldest room. People who have heroic faith are people who genuinely care for other people, and their actions prove it. Some might call it "faith in action."

Heroic Christians may appear to be larger than life, but they really aren't. Yet something about the quality of their faith inspires and motivates us to be more like them. By digesting the above mentioned core values, they have discovered a growth potential that they might not otherwise have known.[4]

WE MUST GET READY TO RAISE OUR SHIELDS AND BECOME GOD'S NEXT GENERATION OF HEROES.

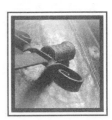

God is still raising up heroes of faith today. Heroes know how to wield their weapons and raise their shields. We must get ready to raise ours and become God's next generation of heroes.

THE BENEFITS OF FAITH

But we are not of those who shrink back to destruction, but of those who have faith to the preserving of the soul. Now faith is the assurance of things hoped for, the conviction of things not seen. For by it the men of old gained approval. . . . And without faith it is impossible to please Him, for he who comes to God must believe that He is, and that He is a rewarder of those who seek Him. . . . By faith Abraham, when he was called, obeyed by going out to a place which he was to receive for an inheritance; and he went out, not knowing where he was going. By faith he lived as an alien in the land of promise, as in a foreign land. . . . By faith even Sarah herself received ability to conceive, even beyond the proper time of life, since she considered Him faithful who had promised (Heb. 10:39—11:11, *NASB*).

This passage lists seven benefits of faith—seven breakthroughs that faith can produce in our lives. Although it is not an exhaustive list, this is a good place to start.

1. Crushes the Strategies of Satan

Hebrews 10:39 informs us, "We are not of those who shrink back to destruction, but of those who have faith to the preserving of the soul."

As we saw in chapter 1 of this book, Satan's goal is to bring us into a place of fear, anxiety, oppression and destruction. Satan wants to raise up mountains of opposition to block our path. He wants to rain down his flaming arrows to intimidate us. He will do everything he can to cause us to shrink back. When we find ourselves in the heat of battle, we don't have to cower in fear. Like Roman soldiers, we can lift up our shields and move forward to obtain the victory. If we turn back, we're in trouble. Faith, however, can equip us to stand against the enemy and keep us on course.

Satan has schemes. The word "conformation" is related to the word "schematic." He will attempt to conform you into his schemes. By faith we can enter into transformation (see Rom. 12:1-2). We can defeat the schemes of the enemy.

2. Brings Us to God

In Hebrews 11:6 we read:

> Without faith it is impossible to please Him, for he who comes to God must believe that He is, and that He is a rewarder of those who seek Him.

We usually think of coming to God in terms of salvation. Abraham believed God and it was counted to him as righteousness. John 3:16 promises that whoever believes in Him will not perish.

But there is more to coming to God than being saved. No matter where we are in our walk with Him, there is always another step. No matter how close to Him we are, there is always more. God calls us to continually seek His presence, and every step toward Him is a step of faith.

3. Induces Movement

Hebrews 11:8 reads: "By faith Abraham, when he was called, obeyed by going out to a place which he was to receive . . . and he went out, not knowing where he was going."

Some people have a call to move out into something but don't have a clue as to where they are going or how they are going to get there. They sit back and say, "When I figure it out, I'll start moving." As a result, they usually never move. There are times when we don't get the clear direction we want from God until we choose to break the inertia—to shake off passivity and just start moving.

Going into new territory involves risk. It is very likely that Abraham was uneasy leaving the beautiful city of Ur and heading out into the wilderness with his wife, servants, flocks and herds. It would have been simpler to stay in Ur and sit around on the couch eating cookies and watching Monday Night Football. Abraham resisted the temptation to take the easy way out and responded to God—even though he didn't know where he was going.

The call to get moving is not a blanket command. We *can* head out into something new and not be obeying God. That's called presumption, which will always get us into a mess. On the other hand, if God says go, then we need to start moving. Getting up off the couch and turning off the television may make us uncomfortable; but if we do not go forward when God tells us to do so, then we risk dying with the TV remote and a tub of popcorn in our hands—a modern equivalent of being in the wilderness.

A few years ago, Robert Heidler and his wife, Linda, went to a Texas Rangers baseball game. Linda is the baseball fan in their family. She carefully watches the game, keeping score and cheering every hit. Robert, on the other hand, spends a lot of time in line at the concession stands. On this occasion, he was waiting to purchase some food when he looked up and saw a message from God. The man in front of him in the line was wearing a T-shirt that read "You can't steal second base with one foot on first." When Robert saw those words, he knew it was a revelation. *That,* he understood, *was faith.*

Stepping out and taking a risk is a dimension of faith that very few people understand. Faith is not just sitting still and waiting for God to do something—although we do need to learn to listen for His voice. That day at the baseball game, God seemed to be telling Robert that faith also involves letting go of what is familiar so that we can move forward to obtain His promises.

That's how Abraham lived. He knew that he could not come into the promise until he left his place of security and started advancing into the unknown.

4. Releases Ability

Hebrews 11:11 reminds us that "by faith even Sarah herself received ability to conceive, even beyond the proper time of life, since she considered Him faithful who had promised."

Faith breaks barrenness. That is part of my wife's testimony. In *The Best Is Yet Ahead,* Pam and I detail the 12 steps that we had to go through to break the spirit of barrenness. God worked in a miraculous way to reverse Pam's barrenness, and we started to have children.[5] Faith can break barrenness in anyone and in any area of life—it does not necessarily have to be physical barrenness.

Some people have lots of kids, but their lives are barren in other ways. Such people often look at their life and see places where the life of God is not flowing. These are areas of what I call dry bones—a grizzly metaphor indeed, but it works. These are areas in which we do not see the things being birthed that need to be birthed.

Faith breaks barrenness. Faith gives us the ability to do what we cannot do naturally; that is why we need to tap the supernatural power of God.

Moses of the Old Testament gave us a great example of how this works. God spoke to him at the burning bush and commissioned him to lead the Israelites. Moses said, "Oh, I can't do that!" (see Exod. 3:11). Many of us can identify with that response.

Barbara Wentroble, who has a wonderful prophetic anointing, shared that when God called her into ministry, she gave Him a long list of reasons why she couldn't do it.

When my coauthor pastor Robert Heidler started college, he was so painfully shy that he could not pray out loud in a group of five or more people.

It is a cliché among Christians but true: We need to be careful when we tell God that we can't do something; He might just go to work on us in that particular area! It doesn't matter what we think we can't do. If we hear the call of God and rise up in faith, we will find that *He can give us the ability to do what we cannot otherwise do.* He will break both physical and spiritual barrenness in our life.

5. Releases Strategy
Hebrews 11:9 says, "By faith [Abraham] lived as an alien in the land of promise, as in a foreign land."

Isn't that verse amazing! Abraham lived as an alien in the land of promise!

We learned a few verses earlier that Abraham went out *not knowing where he was going.* Abraham didn't know where he was going, *yet he made it to the Promised Land!*

WHEN WE TRUST GOD AND BEGIN TO MOVE FORWARD, GOD WILL SHOW US THE WAY!

When you trust God and begin to move forward, God will show you the way! You don't have to have everything figured out in advance.

If you are walking by faith, you can make mistakes along the way. Abraham messed up a number of times. God said, *"Leave your family* and go to the place I'll show you." Abraham *took his family with him,* made it halfway to the Promised Land and then camped out in Haran for a number of years! Along the way Abraham also took a few detours down into Egypt. Abraham made a lot of mistakes, but he had *faith!* Because he had faith, God found a way to get him to the goal.

You might have a promise over your life but not have any idea how to get there. That's okay. God has a way. Strategy and creativity come by faith. If you will link up with God *by faith* and hold on to His promises, He can give you the strategy to see every promise fulfilled.

6. Brings Approval

Hebrews 11:2 reads, "By [faith] the men of old gained approval." It was by faith that the men of old gained God's favor. Using our faith and raising our shields are the only ways to get close to God. We can fast; we can pray; we can try to lead better lives. We can promise God we will do better. We can turn over so many new leaves that we turn into a tree. None of these acts will release God's favor.

What counts is faith.

Robert shared the following with me:

I remember, years ago, hearing the late Dr. Bill Bright give his testimony. Bill Bright was the founder of Campus Crusade for Christ. God used him in incredible ways. He was responsible for hundreds of thousands of people coming to know Jesus as their Savior. He had to trust God to bring in millions of dollars. In his testimony, Dr. Bright told the secret of how he came into the favor of God. As a young man he desired to serve God and be effective for Him more than anything else in the world. He wanted the favor and anointing of God upon his life. He did everything he could think of to gain God's favor. He spent long hours in the Word, long hours in prayer and many days in fasting. In his testimony, he explains how he persevered in these things day after day and month after month, trying to get favor with God. Then, at the end of his testimony, Dr. Bright simply said this, "Then one day I discovered *it is all of faith.*"

The favor and blessing of God do not come through striving, trying, promising or fasting. Those acts all have their place, but what brings the favor of God is faith.

Without faith it is impossible to please God. If it is not of faith, it is sin.

7. Obtains the Promise

Let's turn again to Hebrews: "There was born of one man . . . as many descendants as the stars of heaven in number, and innumerable as the sand which is by the seashore" (11:12).

God promised Abraham that he would be the father of many. Yet in the natural realm there was no way for Abraham to get there. Both Abraham and Sarah were too old to have a child. Yet because they walked in faith, the promise became reality, even though they had to wait 25 more years after the promise to see it fulfilled.

If we believe, we will receive.

You have a promise over your life! It is your call from God. It is part of the purpose for which you were created. God's word to you today is this: *If you believe, you will receive!*

BLESSINGS: A BENEFIT OF FAITH

We often go for long periods of time—or maybe throughout a lifetime—without realizing that we have incredible blessings that God intends for us to receive. I remember when the Lord first showed me this truth. I had just had a great revelation of sin and how it operates through the generations. The Lord had given me faith to break the power of sin. However, I had never seen demonstrated the faith to enter into all the blessings of God. I understood generational sin but not generational blessing.

I had become disciplined in Bible study and prayer. I was devouring the Word of God. At this time in my life, I worked as an executive for one of the major energy companies in downtown Houston. On my hour commute, riding a bus to my workplace, I would read and study the Word. One day as I was riding home, I was reading from Ephesians: "Blessed be the God and Father of our Lord Jesus Christ, who has blessed us with every spiritual blessing in the heavenly places in Christ, just as He chose us in Him before the foundation of the world, that we should be holy and without blame before Him In love" (1:3-4). All of a sudden I felt a quaking inside of me. Something else happened, too. It seemed to me that the heavens opened; and even though I was riding on an earthly bus, my body, soul and spirit were connected into a heavenly realm. Through this opening I saw the blessings God had planned for the generations before me. Even though those generations had not attained all the blessings the Lord showed me, they were still there for me.

He then showed me the blessings He had for me in my present earthly time frame—my life on Earth also had great blessings attached to it. He then showed me the blessings He had planned for my children. This was amazing, because we had been told by doctors that we would not be able to have children. However, I saw the blessings on them in heavenly places. All of a sudden the stirring inside of me felt like an explosion. I said to the Lord, "What is going on?" It seemed as if He impressed me with a loud voice, "I am releasing My faith in you!" I felt like I had so much faith inside that I would explode and turn over the bus I was riding in! I then said to the Lord, "What do I do with this faith?" He replied, "Give it away."

This is how I came to understand the vastness of God's blessings and that once we see the blessings that God has for us, we can attain those blessings by faith.

BE BLESSED

When we think of the biblical concept of blessing, we find that we are called to bless God, that God blesses men and women, that we have the authority to bless one another and that we can even bless things and initiatives. We also use the word "blessing" many times as a salutation or greeting. We send this word by messengers. We use it to extend congratulations for prosperity. We also use "blessings" when we are expressing gratitude. In the New Testament, "blessing" conveys the idea of religious joy that people experience because they are receiving benefits from the kingdom of God.

Jesus used the word "blessed" in the Beatitudes of the Sermon on the Mount (see Matt. 5:3-11). He said that if we would respond positively by faith to the kingdom of God, we would be blessed. We also find in Romans 4:7 that "blessed are those whose lawless deeds have been forgiven, and whose sins have been covered." The apostle John said that we would even be blessed by just reading the book of Revelation (see Rev. 1:3). Probably the most famous concept of blessing comes in Deuteronomy 28 where we find that we can choose blessing.

The Lord is the source of all blessing, and once we express gratitude for His blessing through worship, faith explodes in us. By faith we can enter into both extending and receiving blessings. "Bless the LORD, O my soul; and all that is within me, bless His holy name. Bless the LORD, O my soul, and forget not of His benefits" (Ps. 103:1-2).

Notes

1. R. T. Kendall, *Believing God* (Charlotte, NC: MorningStar Publications, 1997), p. 14.
2. Trevor Newport, *Absolute Faith!* (Chichester, England: New Wine Press, 2000), p. 7.
3. Chuck D. Pierce and Rebecca Wagner Sytsema, *Possessing Your Inheritance* (Ventura, CA: Renew, 1999).
4. The Voice of the Martyrs, *Heroic Faith: How to Live a Life of Extreme Devotion* (Nashville, TN: W Publishing Group, 2002), pp. xv-xvi. Used by permission.
5. Chuck D. Pierce and Rebecca Wagner Sytsema, *The Best Is Yet Ahead* (Colorado Springs, CO: Wagner Publications, 2001).

CHAPTER 4

ENEMIES OF FAITH

God has given us a shield against every attack of the enemy. This shield is activated when we walk in faith. It is then that Jesus takes upon Himself every arrow Satan launches, and Jesus leads us into the fullness of God's blessing. Walking in faith, however, isn't always easy. In fact, there is a battle for faith, and it's a battle each of us must fight.

It is wise to know the schemes of the enemy so that we can be better prepared to enter this battle and win. I introduced the diabolical plotting of Satan in chapter 1. He can be so sly, suggesting certain thoughts and prompting emotions—he is much like C. S. Lewis portrayed Him in his brilliant work *The Screwtape Letters*.

These attacks from Satan can be manifested in many ways. In this chapter we will take a more in-depth look at common ways the enemy will attempt to twist our emotions and actions and, thereby, undercut our faith.

THE REAL BATTLE STARTS

Many Christians do not understand spiritual warfare. They think they are battling for their personal needs. They say, "I'm confronting the enemy because I want a physical healing"; "I'm in a spiritual warfare to break through for financial provision"; "I'm warring in prayer for a new job." In reality, none of these is the object, or goal, of our battle. If we think we are in warfare for healing, money or any other need, perhaps we do not fully understand the battle. Our battle is a battle for faith. The Word of God paints a clear picture: *Faith is essential.* If we have faith, then nothing is impossible, nothing is withheld (see John 16:23-24).

All things are possible if we believe. Faith produces favor; favor opens doors. Therefore, when we have a need for health, money or anything else, our battle is to find a way to stand in faith with our shield lifted. No matter what we need, if we activate our faith, every need will be met.

Life and Death
The battle for faith is a battle for life and death. It involves a warring for the revelation and wisdom we need in each circumstance of life.

God promised the Israelites the land of Canaan (see Deut. 32:49). Even though the Jewish people had to go through the wilderness, they were not to be held captive to the wilderness or die there. The will of God for them was to stay focused until they entered into their promise. They were to overcome any enemy that would hinder them from experiencing the blessings God intended. We know the story: Of the initial group of Jewish people who left Egypt only Caleb and Joshua actually reached the Promised Land. Why? Because the members of the initial group were overcome by fear and unbelief—the wilderness became their home.

SATAN'S SECRET WEAPONS

We have an enemy who is opposing the demonstration of our faith in a holy God. This enemy of faith has a voice. That voice produces a strategy that leads us out of faith and into defeat. That voice creates weapons against faith. Let's uncover those weapons and see how we can raise our shield to quench any word of his that could lead us into unbelief.

How Satan Strikes with Fear

Satan loves to attack faith with fear. Fear encompasses a broad range of emotions that embrace both the secular and the religious worlds. Secular fear is the natural feeling of alarm caused by the expectation of imminent danger, pain or disaster. Religious fear is the result of awe and reverence toward a supreme power. While natural fear is an emotion that human beings exhibit, sometimes fear is a spirit that can hinder and prevent us from advancing into God's plan for our life. Before we can stand against fear, we need to understand what faith is and contrast it with fear.

- Faith is an *expectation* that God is *faithful*.
  It expects that God will keep His promise.

Fear is exactly the opposite.

• Fear is an *expectation* that God will *not* be faithful.
It expects that God will *not* keep His promise.

We all go though difficult times in life. During those difficult times the enemy tries to gain an upper hand or a foothold
against us. I enjoyed reading a book titled *The Gift of Fear* by
Gavin De Becker. In his book De Becker explains how to use the
emotion of fear to our benefit:

> The very fact that you fear something is solid evidence
> that it is not happening. Fear summons powerful pre-
> dictive resources that tell us what might come next. It is
> that which might come next that we fear—what might
> happen, not what is happening now. An absurdly literal
> example helps demonstrate this: As you stand near the
> edge of a high cliff, you might fear getting too close. If
> you stand right at the edge, you no longer fear getting
> too close, you now fear falling . . . [then] if you do fall,
> you no longer fear falling—you fear landing. . . . Panic,
> the great enemy of survival, can be perceived as an
> unmanageable kaleidoscope of fears.
>
> What you fear is rarely what you think you fear—it is
> what you link to fear. Take anything about which you
> have ever felt profound fear and link it to each of the
> possible outcomes. When it is real fear, it will either be in
> the presence of danger, or it will link to pain or death.
> When we get a fear signal, our intuition has already
> made many connections. To best respond, bring the
> links into consciousness and follow them to their high-
> stakes destination—if they lead there. When we focus on
> one link only, say, fear of someone walking toward us on
> a dark street instead of fear of being harmed by someone

walking toward us on a dark street, the fear is wasted. That's because many people will approach us—only a very few might harm us. Surveys have shown that ranking very close to the fear of death is the fear of public speaking. Why would someone feel profound fear, deep in his or her stomach, about public speaking, which is so far from death? Because it isn't so far from death when we link it. Those who fear public speaking actually fear the loss of identity that attaches to performing badly, and that is firmly rooted in our survival needs.[1]

How Fear Works Against Us

Satan takes advantage of us during times of testing. When we come into a time of testing, Satan will try to plant an *expectation* in our heart that God will fail us. When we attempt to stand on God's promises, Satan—à la Lewis's *Screwtape Letters*—will whisper, "You can't count on God to do that!" Satan has many ways of conveying this to us. He has his own version of spiritual gifts. He will use visions, thoughts, and advice we receive from other people. He will tap news reports, music and physical symptoms. He will put us in emotional turmoil to keep us in fear. Let's look at some of the ways Satan can do this.

Satan will give us false visions. We will see vivid pictures in our mind of what it will be like when God fails to keep His promise. A number of years ago, Robert had a serious back injury. He was flat on his back for a month, and every movement brought excruciating pain. As I noted in chapter 1, during this time, he was engaged in a battle. Satan would fill his mind with negative visions to quench his faith for healing. He would see himself in future years, ministering from a wheelchair. Satan would whisper that people would be so impressed that he ministered from a wheelchair, his ministry would be more effective. If he had accepted Satan's vision, Robert might be in a wheelchair now. But he knew that was *not* what God had in mind. Each time Satan brought this vision, Robert stood against the suggestion by focusing on the promises of God. At the end of a month, God sent a friend to pray over Robert's back, and Robert was miraculously healed!

Satan will use news reports. Not long ago, Robert counseled a woman who was out of work. She was filled with fear because she heard on the news that the jobs in her field were drying up. Robert assured her that the news report had nothing to do with God's promise. If there were no available jobs in her field in the entire world, God could still provide for her needs. When she chose to walk in faith, God did provide a job for her in her field—and it was far beyond her expectations. God is not limited by news reports.

Satan will use false symptoms. We may receive prayer for healing and sense a real physical change. But a few days later we feel a twinge of pain and Satan says, "See, it didn't last!" As we are overwhelmed by fear, our faith goes out the window. When we give in to fear, we lower our shield of faith and Satan brings his flaming arrows against us.

Satan will use our weariness. In the book *The Best Is Yet Ahead*, Rebecca Sytsema and I wrote about how we can continue to progress in our prophetic destiny. I wrote that book when I was experiencing a very severe illness. I am an overcomer. I resist the enemy with all of my faculties. However, in times of weakness Satan finds ways to wear down our mind.

Daniel had a very revealing vision in which he is watching an enemy power make war against the saints and prevail against them (see Daniel 7). In this case, "prevail" means to wear down our minds. This is an interesting principle because it shows us that in the midst of our warfare, the enemy is trying to convince us that he will win. During my time of sickness, the enemy showed me the worst scenario. Because of my weariness I was willing to entertain this lie from the enemy. I cried for help from the Lord. I initiated a very close inner circle of friends to surround me with their shield of faith. Then I shared what the

SATAN HAS MANY STRATEGIES TO MAKE US FEARFUL AND THEY ARE ALL DESIGNED TO DESTROY OUR FAITH.

enemy was saying to me. Once I had spoken, my wife, Pam, gave a word from God that negated the enemy's voice. The point is this: Even though I was weary and the enemy was taking advantage of my weakness, others who had their faith shield in place came to my rescue.

Why We Fear Horses

Satan has many strategies to make us fearful and they are all designed to destroy our faith. Satan will fill us with fear to make us put down our shield of faith. When we give in to fear, we are no longer operating in faith. Every one of us has a choice. We can choose to accept the fear Satan is trying to plant in our mind or we can decide to stand in faith and trust God. Fear not! Genesis 15:1 (*KJV*) gives us all the advice we need:

> After these things the word of the LORD came unto Abram in a vision, saying, Fear not, Abram: I am thy shield, and thy exceeding great reward.

God spoke this to Abraham before He began to fully make covenant with him and the generations to come. He knew that fear would be an issue Abraham would have to contend with. However, God said, "I will shield you in the midst of the enemy's plan to keep you from advancing into the fullness of this promise that I am about to give you" (see Gen. 15:1).

If we will let the spirit of fear that is taunting us know that God is our shield, then our faith will manifest in a great reward. In his book *Breaking Intimidation*, John Bevere wrote that we tend to serve whatever we fear:

> The church does not understand the fear of the Lord. This is unfortunate because it is a significant element to a triumphant Christian life. Isaiah prophesied concerning Jesus, "His delight is in the fear of the Lord" (Isa. 11:3). His delight should be ours! The man who fears God will be led in God's ways (Ps. 25:12). That man "shall dwell in prosperity, and his descendants shall inherit the earth" (v. 13) . . . the fear of the Lord is the beginning of wisdom and the beginning of knowledge of Him (Prov. 9:10; 1:7; 2:5). It will prolong our days (Prov. 10:27). We are warned that no one will see the Lord without holiness which is perfected by the fear of the Lord (Heb. 12:14; 2 Cor. 7:1). And this is just a sampling of what the Bible says about the fear of the Lord. The only way to walk totally free from intimidation is to walk in the fear of the Lord.
>
> To fear man is to stand in alarm, anxiety, awe, dread and suspicion, cowering before mortal men. When entrapped by this fear we will live on the run, hiding from harm or reproach, and constantly avoiding rejection and confrontation. We become so busy

safeguarding ourselves and serving men that we are ineffective in our service for God. Afraid of what man can do to us, we will not give God what He deserves. The Bible tells us, "The fear of man brings a snare" (Prov. 29:18). A snare is a trap. Fearing man steals our God-given authority. His gift then lies dormant in us. We feel powerless to do what is right because the empowering of God is inactive.[2]

Psalm 34:4 underscores Bevere's insight: "I sought the LORD, and He heard me, and delivered me from all my fears." This verse declares that God will save us from all our fears. In *They Shall Expel Demons*, Derek Prince shared the many different kinds of fear:

Fear of the dark, fear of heights, fear of man, fear of failure, fear of sickness, fear of death, fear of confined places (claustrophobia), fear of open or public places (agoraphobia), (and) fear of the unknown.[3]

One time when I was speaking at a church, I called people forward who had a fear of horses. I was so surprised when more than 150 of the 800 people in attendance came up for prayer. My text was Jeremiah 12:5: "If you have run with the footmen, and they have wearied you, then how can you contend with horses?" I realized that many people could not move forward in their lives because they had fear. So I used this Scripture to say, "How many of you have a fear of horses? The horses in this Scripture represent the troubles ahead. You can never advance to contend with the 'horses' if you have fear of the troubles ahead." Many times our fear of something in particular represents our general fear of the future.

How Doubt Attacks

Satan likes to fill us with doubt. To accomplish this he plants questions in our mind about the goodness and love of God. When Satan approached Eve in the garden, his strategy was to cause her to doubt God's goodness. He insinuated that God did not have her best interest at heart and that God was trying to keep her from what would be best for her.

Doubt is linked to indecision. Doubt means that we are inclined to disbelief. Doubt occurs when we waver between two opinions. The dictionary defines doubt with terms such as "hesitate," "question," "to be uncertain about," "inclined to disbelief," "fearful," "apprehensive or suspicious in such a way that you are not certain about your choice or way ahead."[4] "Doubtful" implies strong uncertainty as to the probability, value, honesty or validity of something.

The most famous person in the Bible who is linked to doubt is Thomas. Jesus had informed His disciples many times that He would die, overcome death and then rise again. Upon rising, Jesus appeared to His disciples. At the tomb, He sent Mary Magdalene and the other women to inform the disciples that He was alive again. In Mark 16 we find that the disciples did not believe; rather, they doubted Mary's word (see Mark 16:11). Because they did not believe, Jesus appeared to them Himself. He actually walked through the wall and shut door of the room in which they were assembled, hiding out in fear. Thomas, however, was not present. Here was Thomas's response when the disciples chose to believe in Jesus' resurrection:

> Unless I see in His hands the print of the nails, and put my finger into the print of the nails, and put my hand into His side, I will not believe (John 20:25).

Eight days later, Jesus stood in their midst again. Thomas was present this time. Jesus said to him, "Reach your finger here, and look at My hands; and reach your hand here, and put it into My

WHEN WE GO THROUGH TRIALS, SATAN TRIES TO PREVENT US FROM ENTERING INTO FAITH.

side. Do not be unbelieving, but believing" (v. 27). This convinced Thomas that the Lord really was who He proclaimed He was and had done what He had proclaimed He would do. The Lord, however, rebuked him: "Blessed are those who have not seen and yet have believed" (v. 29).

When we go through trials, Satan tries to prevent us from entering into faith. Our skepticism might cause us to question the goodness of God. We might say, "Yes, God healed Hector and he healed Stephanie, but He won't do that for me." Satan knows that if he can get us to doubt God's goodness, then our shield of faith will be deactivated. We must watch for Satan's attempts to plant that doubt. If we are going through a trial and find ourselves thinking, *I don't see why God would allow this if He is good,* then we can be sure we have just heard the voice of Satan. If Satan can *fill us with fear* and from that fear cause us to begin to *doubt God's goodness,* then Satan can begin to destroy our faith.

Doubt is a product of unbelief. Doubt will harden our hearts. Our unbelief will then become a self-fulfilling prophecy. If we allow ourselves to walk in unbelief, we are *choosing* to experience the lack of God's provision. God promised Israel a wonderful land flowing with milk and honey. But the initial generation that left Egypt *chose to believe* they would die in the wilderness. Because they did not believe God's promise to them would be fulfilled, they received what they believed. They died in the wilderness.

As we go through our wilderness, Satan will raise up a mountain of fear and doubt to block our way. That fear and doubt will keep us in the wilderness until we overcome it. Just as Alison Krauss's wonderful song (see the page opposite the opening of chapter 1) declares, we can end up dying in the wilderness if we do not stand against the voice of unbelief and learn to raise high our shield of faith.

Notes

1. Gavin De Becker, *The Gift of Fear* (New York: Dell Publishing, 1997), pp. 341-342.
2. John Bevere, *Breaking Intimidation* (Lake Mary, FL: Creation House, 1995), pp. 141-142.
3. Derek Prince, *They Shall Expel Demons* (Grand Rapids, MI: Baker Book House, 1998), p. 79.
4. *Merriam-Webster's Collegiate Dictionay*, 10th ed., s.v. "doubt."

CHAPTER 5

THE POWER OF OUR WORDS

Satan's number one goal is to cause our shield of faith to be useless. If he can discredit the object of our faith, then we will lay down our shield and question the worth of the battle itself.

In the previous chapter, I explained Satan's primary weapons for undermining our faith: fear and doubt. Sometimes, however, we participate with the enemy through the power of our words. The power of our words can either make or destroy our faith. Through murmuring, or complaining, we fall prey to the enemy's plan. I like to define "murmuring" and "complaining" as repeatly voicing our dissatisfaction over the situation God has placed us in.

Now the people became like those who complain of adversity in the hearing of the Lord; and when the Lord heard it, His anger was kindled, and the fire of the Lord burned among them (Num. 11:1, NASB).

Now these things happened as examples for us, that we should not crave evil things, as they also craved. . . . Nor let us try the Lord, as some of them did, . . . nor grumble, as some of them did, and were destroyed by the destroyer (1 Cor. 10:6-10, *NASB*).

When we're in the wilderness, the greatest snare to which we can fall prey is to murmur, or complain, about our present situation rather than looking ahead to the place God has for us. This was certainly true for Israel. They grumbled from the moment they were delivered out of Egypt and slavery. During every test in the wilderness their response was to murmur, or complain. This, as I have already noted, is what ultimately kept them out of the Promised Land.

SATAN'S WEAPON OF MURMURING

A lot of people don't look at murmuring, or complaining, like something bad. For many of us, complaining is our favorite pastime. We get together with a friend and say, "Let me tell you what bad thing happened to me." Then the friend says, "I can top that! Wait till you hear what happened to *me!*" Soon our fellowship has turned into a full-blown pity party.

Most of us think pity parties are normal. God, however, wants us to know that He hates complaining. He doesn't take it lightly. Read Numbers 11:1, given above, and then carefully look over these verses:

How long shall I bear with this evil congregation? . . . I have heard the murmurings which the children of Israel murmur against Me (Num. 14:27).

Do not harden your hearts as when they provoked Me, as in the day of trial in the wilderness. . . . Take care, brethren, lest there should be in any one of you an evil, unbelieving heart (Heb. 3:8-12, *NASB*).

Many times we start moving toward the promise God has for us—and we may even break out of some type of bondage—but then we stop. We get stuck. We *allow* Satan to interfere and stop our progress. (In chapter 7, I write about overcoming the enemy's blockades.) We forget about our deliverance and the joy we have experienced in the past, and we begin to murmur, or complain.

The Root of Bitterness

Sometimes complaining issues from bitterness. Bitterness has a definite progression. Perhaps you have prayed and are still struggling with a particular problem in your life. What do you

WHEREVER THERE IS COMPLAINING, YOU CAN BE SURE THAT FAITH IS NO LONGER PRESENT.

do next? You get angry with God! You tell someone (everyone who will listen!) how upset you are about the situation. Most of us have done this at one time or another. When we do, we usually seek sympathy but often land in self-pity.

Murmuring arises out of what I call a heart of bitterness and is a weapon in the arsenal of the enemy. Wherever there is complaining, you can be sure that faith is no longer present.

One of the greatest examples of bitterness of heart is found in Naomi's story. The book of Ruth tells us about the restoration of Naomi's inheritance.[1] At the beginning of the book of Ruth, we find that Naomi has reason to be bitter: She has lost everything. At first she blames God for those things that have been stolen, killed and destroyed—what was supposed to be her inheritance. Naomi's name should mean pleasant, delightful and lovely, but she becomes known as Marah, or bitter. To be bitter means to have a sharp, disagreeable taste. This taste is a reflection of sorrow, discomfort, pain or injustice. The beauty of the book of Ruth lies in how God leads Naomi out of bitterness and restores her to pleasantness through her covenant relationship with Ruth.

James 3:14 reads, "But if you have bitter envy and self-seeking [selfish ambition] in your hearts, do not boast and lie against the truth." The context of this passage is that of a teacher instructing with wisdom. Bitterness and envy go hand in hand. This combination produces confusion and every evil thing.

> Pursue peace with all men and holiness, without which no one will see the Lord: looking diligently lest anyone fall short of the grace of God; lest any root of bitterness springing up cause trouble, and by this many become defiled (Heb. 12:14-15).

This verse is a warning that bitterness can cause us to leave the faith. Bitterness can become a root that not only defiles our whole body but also defiles God's corporate purpose, which we are a part of. Israel as a whole became infected with bitterness in the wilderness, and because of it a whole generation was unable to enter into the promise. When we are struggling in the area of murmuring, or complaining, we must allow God to remove the bitterness and restore our pleasant fragrance.

The Dangers of Murmuring

The Bible reveals that complaining, or murmuring, is dangerous for at least four reasons:

1. *Murmuring cuts off our vision for the future.* Jesus did not murmur and complain on the cross because His eyes were fixed on the outcome: "For the joy that was set before Him endured the cross, despising the shame" (Heb. 12:2). We don't complain in the wilderness if our eyes are on the promised land! Our problem is that Satan tells us there is no way out of the wilderness. Satan tells us "You will die in the wilderness—there's no way out!" God says, "Follow Me! I have a promised land for you!" We get to choose who we're going to agree with! When we complain, we are agreeing with the devil that our future is cut off.

2. *Murmuring is dangerous because it causes us to doubt God's goodness for the present.* When we complain, we are saying, "God, I don't like the route You have mapped for my life." Romans 8:28 teaches that God has a route planned for us. All of the things on that route—even those that are not fun—are designed by God to work together for our good. When we complain, we are saying, "God, I don't like this route. I don't think You've done a good job." Murmuring is an accusation against God that His plan for us is not a good plan.

3. *Murmuring causes unbelief to deepen and grow.* The Lord told me something awhile back. He said, "Unbelief is like a seed; if you water it, it will grow." Every time we complain, we are *watering* our unbelief. What happens when you are underwater and open your mouth wide? Water comes in! In the same way, when we open our mouth to complain, unbelief floods in. If we are having a hard time walking in faith and we open our mouth to complain, we have just lost the battle because we have opened ourselves to a flood of unbelief. Sometimes the best thing we can do to stay in faith is just to shut our mouth!

4. *Murmuring invites greater adversity.* Some of us have gotten into a cycle that gets worse and worse! When we're having a problem with someone and we complain, what happens? We experience more adversity. Murmuring puts us under a curse. Let me prove this from Scripture. What was Israel's complaint in the wilderness? The Jewish people said, "We are going to die in the wilderness!" That was not God's plan. He had promised to get them to the Promised Land.

> Then the LORD spoke to Moses and Aaron, saying "How long shall I bear with this evil congregation who murmur against Me? I have heard the murmurings which the children of Israel murmur against Me. Say to them, 'As I live,' says the LORD, 'just as you have spoken in My hearing, so I will do to you: The carcasses of you who have murmured against Me shall fall in this wilderness'" (Num. 14:27-29).

What was God was saying? "You have refused to come into agreement with My words over your life, so instead I will come into agreement with your words." We must be careful about what we say.

THE ALTERNATIVE TO MURMURING

Some of us have gotten so used to complaining that it's hard to do anything else. After all, what else can we do in the wilderness but complain? Isaiah 61 gives the answer. We can put on a mantle of praise (see v. 3). A mantle is like a cape or a topcoat. It is something we *choose* to put on. And we can choose to put it on in any situation.

I think the best example of this is when God gave Paul a vision and told him to go to Philippi. Paul got there, but after a brief time of ministry, he was arrested. His robes were torn off and he was beaten. He was struck with many blows and thrown into prison, where his feet were put in stocks. The stocks were not to keep Paul from escaping; the guards and the bars would do that. The stocks were a method of torture. The stocks forced him to spend the night lying on his back in agony.

Paul had done nothing wrong. Not only was this treatment unfair, but it also was illegal. The rulers of the day did not allow their own citizens to undergo such humiliation.

It might be understandable if a person in such a situation responded in anger, don't you think? But how did Paul react? He sang praise songs!

Did Paul *feel* full of praise at the moment? Not at all! I believe that Paul said, "I'm going to put on my mantle of praise. I feel miserable, and I can't sleep because of the pain, but I'm going to fill this cell with the praises of God!"

We can also *choose* to do that in any situation! Praise is our shield against unbelief. Praise guards us against complaining. If

IF THERE IS PRAISE COMING OUT OF OUR MOUTHS, THERE IS NO ROOM FOR COMPLAINING.

we feel like complaining, then we can choose instead to praise God. If there is praise coming out of our mouths, there is no room for complaining.

How can we praise God in the wilderness? Here are four suggestions:

1. *We can learn to praise God in adversity.* Robert and his wife, Linda, have found this to be true on mission trips. On their first venture to Ukraine, Linda went into the bathroom to wash her face. Just as she got it all soapy, the water stopped coming out of the faucet. Linda learned new praise. The next day, when she turned on the faucet and water came out, it was something for which she could praise God. There are many things we take for granted until we don't have them.

2. *We can praise God for His goodness.* Even when God has us in the wilderness, there are blessings for which we can praise Him. When Israel was in the wilderness, they received manna (bread) from heaven. It came every day. Their shoes did not wear out for 40 years. They saw the visible *shekinah* glory of God leading them as a pillar of cloud by day and as a pil-

lar of fire by night. God's goodness is not cut off from us in the wilderness. We need to take our eyes off he discomfort of our situation and look around us. We will surely find things for which we can offer praise.

3. *We can praise God for His presence.* No matter what wilderness we are in, God is in it with us. His presence is there. When Robert's back was out for a month, he could not move without excruciating pain. He spent that month lying on his back, holding the Bible and reading the Word. During that time the presence of God came down and met with him. He had some of the closest times with the Lord he's ever had in his life. When we are in the wilderness, God is there to meet with us. Begin to praise Him for His presence.

4. *We can praise God for the outcome.* No matter what wilderness we are in, God has a plan for us through that wilderness, and it is a plan to take us into a place of promise.

Jeremiah 29:11 (*NASB*) records God's words: "'For I know the plans I have for you,' declares the LORD, 'plans for welfare and not for calamity to give you a future and a hope.'" God always has a promised outcome.

When we are in the midst of the test, we can say, "Lord, I praise You! I thank You for this opportunity to trust You. Lord, I thank You for the outcome—for the blessings You will bring me through this test!"

When we choose to praise instead of complain, unbelief is cut off. At that very moment we are enabled to lift up our shield of faith and receive the promise.

SATAN'S WEAPON OF SELF-PITY

If we see that offering praise counteracts murmuring a complaint we can choose to praise rather than complain, but it is not always that clear-cut. Sometimes we have fallen into a cycle of self-pity that has its origin in deep pain. Once we get wounded or experience loss, we can lose sight of our future. This leads to a battle with self-pity, which Satan uses to prevent us from seeing God's glory manifest itself in our life. Self-pity is a demonic force that draws attention to our loss. Instead of seeing God's continued perfect plan for our life, self rises up and says, "Pity me for what I have lost." Any time we experience loss, trauma, wounding or injustice, our mind-set can go in two directions: We can live believing that God can heal and forgive, or our thoughts can form around attitudes of rejection, self-defense and self-pity.

SATAN'S OTHER WEAPONS

Satan eagerly uses any weapon that will be effective against us. Among these are anger, delusion and the fear of death.

Anger

As we move forward in our spiritual life, we must guard against the presence of anger or bitterness in our hearts. Ephesians 4:26 is an admonishment from Paul to the people of Ephesus to "'be angry, and do not sin': do not let the sun go down on your wrath, nor give place to the devil." Anger may win the moment, but it won't win the war. Anger is a peculiar emotion. The Lord doesn't tell us we can't be angry; however, if we don't manage our anger, we can actually give ground in our life to satanic control. Demons can vex and oppress us. Instead of our possessing the best that God has for us, we lose ground. Anger can never be a part of our shield of faith. Anger produces jealousy; jealousy leads to hate; hate devises destruction and eventually produces a murderous act, whether by word or deed.

Emotions are God given, but unless we express our emotions in healthy ways, we will never accomplish God's plan for our life. In *A Woman's Guide to Breaking Bondages*, Quin Sherrer and Ruthanne Garlock wrote:

> Anger is perhaps hardest to handle, especially if we have stored it up only to overreact to only a relatively minor infraction . . . because stored-up anger becomes corrosive and dangerous. It's like putting a tempest in a teapot; if not calmed it's bound to cause destruction. Anger almost always begins with a perceived loss, an actual loss or the threat of loss. The loss itself, coupled with the feeling that we are being victimized, produces anger.[2]

Anger changes the chemical makeup of the body. When anger is present, adrenaline—a hormone produced by the adrenal glands—is released. The release of this hormone produces a fight-or-flight response, which is a good response when you are in danger. However, as a response to anger, the continuous release of adrenaline can be physically damaging to our body. We need to give the management of our anger—or any negative emotion—to the Holy Spirit's control for the good of mind, body and spirit.

Delusion

As noted earlier, by believing just one lie, we lose the reality of God in our life. Satan's plan is to delude us; he longs to mislead, beguile, frustrate and deceive us. If we ever embrace a single lie, then we can eventually end up in total delusion. A delusion is a false belief or opinion that is contrary to fact or reality and results in a nervous or mental disorder. Satan's ultimate goal is to use delusion to remove the reality of God from our life and testimony. Isaiah 66:4 reads:

> So will I choose their delusions, and bring their fears on them; because, when I called, no one answered, when I spoke they did not hear; but they did evil before My eyes, and chose that in which I do not delight.

This verse says that God will allow that delusion to come upon us. Before long we will not be able to discern right and from wrong. A spirit of delusion blinds our conscience and keeps us from making wise choices because our choices are based on the delusion we have embraced.

Delusion is also linked with desire; desire is a function of the emotions. When we allow our emotions to control us, our desire can lead us into disaster. Second Thessalonians 2:11-12 records:

> And for this reason God will send them strong delusion, that they should believe the lie, that they all may be condemned who did not believe the truth but had pleasure in unrighteousness.

In both the Isaiah and 2 Thessalonians passages, the word "delusion" is used; it implies that unbridled desire has been embraced. That is when God sends the delusion. Another way to understand "delusion" is to understand the word "error," which is linked with the word "planet." In other words, we go so far astray from God's purpose in respect to morals and doctrine that figuratively we end up on another planet. I have seen people who have such a strong desire in one area of their life—whether for a mate, for money or for power—that they end up with their faith totally shipwrecked. They have followed after a lie that has led them into delusion.

Death

One of the enemy's most successful strategies is to make us fearful of death. In fact, he would nag us to death about death if he could. Even though death is our final enemy and we all will face

ONE OF THE ENEMY'S MOST SUCCESSFUL STRATEGIES IS TO MAKE US FEARFUL OF DEATH.

it at some point, we do not have to live in bondage to that fear. I declare that every strategy in which Satan has convinced someone of premature death will be broken.

Romans 6:23 reads, "The wages of sin is death." Without Jesus we can fear death because we have all sinned and we all deserve death. Jesus, however, made a provision when He died on the cross. When we accept Him as Savior, the "wages of sin" are forgiven because Jesus took that debt upon Himself for us. Thank God we have an advocate to break this enemy of death. If anyone has experienced the sting of death in their life and that sting has affected their faith, then they should ask the Lord to put His healing touch upon the sting.

OUR WEAPON AGAINST THE ENEMY

A major weapon in the battle for faith is the Word of God. Proverbs 18:21 reads, "Death and life are in the power of the tongue." God's *rhema,* or spoken word, is key to our liberation. This is the word that God has spoken about our situation. God's rhema is the sword of the Spirit (see Eph. 6:17). God has given us His Word as a sword to use against the voice of the enemy. When Satan attacks our faith, we do not have to sit there and let him batter us with fear and doubt until we die. God has put a sword in our hand to drive back the enemy.

If we want to see how to use our sword, look at Jesus! When Jesus was in the wilderness, Satan came to tempt Him. In each temptation, Satan's goal was to make Jesus doubt the goodness of God's plan. Satan said in effect, "You don't have to die on the Cross! That's not a good plan! Just worship me and I'll give You the kingdoms of the world!"

In response to these attacks, Jesus pulled out His sword. Every time Satan tried to plant doubt about God's goodness, Jesus' answered, "No, Satan! For it is written" (see Luke 4:4,8,10). Jesus jabbed Satan with God's Word until Satan went away!

We can do likewise. God has put a sword in our hand! Every time Satan comes to stick us with his sword of fear and unbelief, we can either sit there and let him jab away or we can take up our sword and fight. We can say, "No, Satan! For it is written." We, too, can remind Satan of what God has promised us.

The Word of God is our weapon against the enemy, yet when we are in the battle, we always have two words to choose from. First, we have a word from God. When people come to me for counseling about a problem, the first question I ask is "Has God spoken to you about this?" Almost invariably, the person knows that indeed God has spoken. God has quickened a verse from Scripture. God has spoken in His still small voice to give this person His promise.

Although we have a word from God—it is His promise in the situation—we also have a word from Satan. How do we tell the difference? A word from Satan can sound very religious—Satan loves to quote Scripture. The difference is that God's word releases faith; Satan's word releases fear, doubt and unbelief. Faith comes by hearing the rhema, the spoken word, of God. Fear and doubt come by hearing the voice of Satan, who is the father of lies.

When we are in battle, it is helpful to stop and discern what both of these voices are saying. Do we know what God is saying to us? Have we heard a word that releases faith? What is Satan saying? How is he trying to fill us with unbelief? Once we have sorted out what each voice is saying, we must then decide which voice to follow. If we choose to agree with God, then we must confront the enemy.

> We must learn to do warfare with our prophecies. "This charge I commit to you, son Timothy, according to the prophecies previously made concerning you, that by them you may wage the good warfare" (1 Tim. 1:18). Receiving a prophetic revelation from God about what He wants to accomplish does not mean that it's a done deal. There is a conditional nature to prophecy that involves both our obedience and our willingness to "war" with a word.[3]

When Satan speaks to us and we sense that mountain of fear and doubt rising up, what then should we do? We must reject it. We cannot just sit there and allow Satan to fill our mind with garbage. When the voice of the enemy comes, we must confront it with God's Word: "No, Satan! I am choosing to believe God. It is written."

As we confront Satan with the Word of God, an amazing thing happens: Faith replaces unbelief! Most Christians think faith is hard to come by. They assume that it's normal to walk in unbelief. That's not true. The natural state of a believer is to believe—faith should flow naturally from our spirit. If we fill our mind with God's Word and refuse to listen to the voice of unbelief, then faith will flow automatically.

Faith is in us through the Spirit of God. The battle for faith is a battle to defeat unbelief. If we will stand against the voice of the enemy, we will see faith replace unbelief.

Here are some keys to increased faith:

1. *Each of us must fill our mind with God's written Word, the Bible.* We must read, meditate on and saturate our mind with what God has said. Out of that we get our ammunition against the enemy. Be in the Word!

   A. As we are in the Word, we need to allow God to show us His character. We need to see the display of His goodness, faithfulness, kindness and strength. That gives that us a foundation to stand on.

   B. As we are in the Word, we can see the ways of God. God has certain ways of doing things. Knowing how God deals with people makes it easier to walk in faith when He's dealing with us!

   C. As we are in the Word, we receive God's rhema, or spoken, word. When we are going through a trial, verses from the Bible will begin to jump off the page for us. God will quicken verses, applying them directly to us. These are rhema, or spoken, words. We must pay attention to what God says and stand on His promises.

2. *We should fill our mind with praise and thankfulness.* Faith is nurtured by maintaining an atmosphere of praise and thanksgiving. If we walk through life in praise and thankfulness, we will find that faith is a natural overflow.

3. *We must trust God where we can.* There's always something we can trust God for. If we feel like we don't have faith to trust God for our present situation, we can back up to where we do have faith and take a stand there. Abraham believed God for a son, and God counted it as righteousness. We must believe where we can.

4. *We need to express our faith in obedience.* Faith must always be expressed. Faith is never just an intellectual exercise. We should express it. We need to ask God how He wants us to express our faith. If we obey God and stay in faith, we will see the breakthrough.

All the fiery darts Satan uses against us—fear, doubt, murmuring, self-pity, anger, delusion and death—can be quenched by our shield of faith.

Notes

1. Rebecca Sytsema and I wrote about this in detail in *Possessing Our Inheritance* (Ventura, CA: Regal Books, 2001).

2. Quin Sherrer and Ruthanne Garlock, *A Woman's Guide to Breaking Bondages* (Ann Arbor, MI: Servant Publications, 1994), pp. 47-48.

3. Chuck D. Pierce and Rebecca Wagner Sytsema, *The Best Is Yet Ahead* (Colorado Springs, CO: Wagner Publications, 2001), p. 67.

CHAPTER 6

PASSING THE TEST

Many times when God is ready to fulfill a promise, we find ourselves in a time of testing. This seems to be a biblical pattern that runs from Genesis to Revelation. Israel—whom we have been using as a model for our spiritual walk in this book—discovered this process of testing in the wilderness. God had promised Abraham the land of Canaan, a land filled with wonderful blessings. That promise had been extended through the generations and became a corporate promise for a nation. However, before the Jewish people could receive the Promised Land blessings, they had to make it through the wilderness testings.

We all go through tests in our own wilderness. This is unavoidable. However, the length of time we spend in the wilderness is determined by how we respond to

God's exam. It was only about a two-year hike from Egypt to the Promised Land (they did not have SUVs in those days). The Jewish people, however, kept failing tests along the way. We know the story: It took them 40 years to make it.

Noah, Esther and Daniel also were tested. Each one passed, but sometimes it took quite a while. Jesus was tested, too. He had been baptized and was ready to fulfill all righteousness, but first He had to pass a test. He went into the wilderness where for 40 days He had to resist the wiles of the devil. When He came out, He had power. Jesus is our model; therefore, we can conclude that we can expect to go through everything He went through. If we pass the test, then we too can expect power.

ENDURING FAITH

Faith is the key to making it through the wilderness. When we are in a time of testing, the issue is always faith. But there is a special kind of faith needed to pass the test and possess the promise: enduring faith. This is a faith that perseveres to the end of the test. By then we have developed a rock-solid testimony.

> But he who endures to the end will be saved. And this gospel of the kingdom will be preached in all the world as a witness to all the nations, and then the end will come (Matt. 24:13-14).

"To endure" (*hupomeno* in Greek) is to hold our ground in conflict, bear up under adversity, hold out under stress, stand firm, persevere or wait calmly and courageously. This implies an energetic resistance to defeat that produces calm and brave perseverance. "Perseverance" is very similar to "endurance," but "perseverance" means to do something in spite of the difficulty, to have a steadfastness or to persist until the purpose is accomplished. If we persevere, we successfully get past the obstacles that are in our path (we will look at faith that moves us past the enemy's blockades in chapter 7). Hebrews 10:36 describes this kind of faith: "You have need of endurance, so that after you have done the will of God, you may receive the promise." James 1:3-4 (*NASB*) puts it this way, "The testing of your faith produces endurance. And let endurance have its perfect result, that you may be perfect and complete, lacking in nothing" (see also Jas. 1:12).

It is easy to receive a promise and become excited. But often by the third day, we have been beset by one attack or another from the enemy. The promise we glowed about on Sunday morning gets nudged to the side and then shoved to the back of our minds. How do we stay on course?

We can begin by looking at the mistakes made by those who did not enter into faith, or did persevere once they got a promise from God. We learn many lessons of what not to do from those who got discouraged and quit rather than pressing on.

THE HEALER REVEALED

The Lord revealed Himself as *Jehovah Rophe*, meaning "Jehovah heals" (see Exod. 15:26). This is the second of the compound names of the Lord's revelation to His covenant people, Israel, the Jewish people. I believe there is a progression in the way that He revealed Himself to His people. There also is a progression in the way God reveals Himself to us. Many times as we attempt to go toward the promise of God, we get bogged down by a circumstance. Instead of crying out for the Lord to reveal Himself to us in our situation, we either rely on our own understanding or murmur and complain (as we've already noted).

Three days after crossing the Red Sea, the people of Israel hit a blockade: No water was available. They murmured and complained. God then revealed Himself to them as a Healer, because they needed healing. They had forgotten the song of triumph they had sung as they crossed the Red Sea.

They did find water, but it was bitter. This mocked their thirst. They grew angry because the expectation that they had of

IN THE MIDST OF OUR TRIALS, GOD PROVES HIMSELF.

quenched thirst had not been met. Expectation, when not fulfilled, produces what I call hope deferred. Expectation is a function of the emotions. When our expectation is not met, our emotions react. We fall into this trap despite God's track record.

What a test! God eventually showed Moses a tree that could turn the bitterness to sweetness—but it took faith. God was proving their faith. God is never on trial. In the midst of our trials, God proves Himself, if we will rely upon Him. We find from this test of God's covenant people that there will be times in our life when we need a Healer.

Some of our greatest trials are related to a spirit of infirmity. This spirit produces weakness. Whether our problem is moral, spiritual or physical, we need a Healer. Sickness takes a great toll on our lives. Disease can produce tremendous confusion and havoc. Disease is no respecter of persons or class. During these time of infirmity, we need the Healer.

God Himself is the One who heals. However, He uses sickness! He has left infirmity present on Earth as an instrument to judge sin and to strengthen our faith. Our tragedy is that many times in the midst of our test we do not see that we need the Healer to intervene.

Many times disappointment, bitterness and hope deferred settle in our emotions. As Proverbs 13:12 declares: "Hope deferred makes the heart sick, but when the desire comes, it is a tree of life." Just as the tree was there for the Jewish people to change the bitter water to sweet, the Lord also has the power—and desire—to heal. Many times the only obstacle lies within us. Perhaps it is an unresolved wound, a bitter heart or faith that will not rise and see the tree in our midst.

Loss and Hope Deferred

Just as infirmity is part of the Christian life, so is loss. In *Possessing Your Inheritance*, Rebecca Sytsema and I wrote:

> Whether it be through death, divorce, job loss, victimiza-tion, disabilities, property loss or a myriad of other tragedies and disappointments, everyone has experienced loss in one form or another. . . . All loss produces some kind of grief, which is the emotional expression of loss. . . . Experts in the field of human behavior tell us there are, in fact, stages to the "normal" grieving process. . . . The griev-ing process affects everyone differently.[1]

Rebecca and I then list two instances in which grief can keep us from moving toward restoration: when the cycle of grief is not completed and when the cycle of grief goes on too long.[2]

During our times of loss we experience emotions such as shock, denial, depression, anger, guilt and confusion. These are all normal emotions that follow a traumatic loss. The enemy attempts to take each one and use it as a fiery dart. He throws it back at us in an attempt to produce a hole in our shield of faith. Even as we resist during these times of loss, our shield of faith can be weakened.

Dangers of Hope Deferred

During loss and wounding, we have a tendency to accuse God for the trauma we are experiencing. The power of this accusation leads to a type of fatherlessness. Instead of experiencing the spirit of adoption, we feel abandoned and lost. From our self-defense we actually form a rebellion to authority. We also become unteachable. We have a mind-set that says, "No one understands me or what I am going through."

We also begin to think there is no solution to our problem. We fall into apathy because we have no hope of healing or restoration. We know we should be living a godly life; therefore, religious mechanisms become a solace to us. We even gain a martyr complex and may say, "O woe is me. This is my cross to bear. Look how heavy is my cross." This type of thinking leads us to not fight when we need to. Instead of fighting and advancing, we become slaves to comfort and the status quo.

We forget that we are called to fellowship with His sufferings. This type of fellowship leads us to His resurrection power manifesting in us. If we ever lose sight of the love of God, we turn to self. God's love forces us to deal with the thoughts that are listed above. I have experienced enough freedom in my own life to know when I am not free. Faith works by love. Once we experience His liberty and love, we will be able to resist that call from self to be pitied and can overthrow hope deferred.[3]

Hope deferred happens when we begin with an expectation that God will break through. We face a test, and our shield of faith is in place, but we have assumed that God would act in a certain way and in a certain time frame. The time we have established comes, but we don't see the answer. The fulfillment of our hope is deferred. We find ourselves continuing to wait for a breakthrough, but as we wait we grow tired and become discouraged. Our heart feels sick. Satan tells us that the breakthrough will never come.

In the midst of hope deferred, our shield of faith seems like a heavy burden to carry. The temptation is to lay it down. But if we let go of our faith, we can miss the promise. It is not enough to start out in faith; we must continue along the path, taking each step in faith. And we must be patient.

Faith + Patience = Promises Received

Many of us have been taught that we receive God's promises by faith. That is true, but it is only half the equation. The Bible teaches that we inherit God's promises through faith *and* *patience*. Faith alone is not enough. We have to have a faith that lasts, a faith that endures, a faith that stands the test. Abraham waited. Jesus waited. We too must learn to wait.

Hope deferred strikes when we allow delay to bring discouragement. Here's how hope deferred operates: We come into a time of testing, so we fix our eyes on God's promises and declare, "I'm going to believe these promises because I know God is faithful."

Ten minutes go by without an answer, so we repeat each step of claiming the promise. Ten hours go by without a response, and we try one more time with vigor and earnestness.

Ten days go by, and we say, "Well, I *guess* I still believe these promises."

Ten weeks go by, and we mumble, "I sure thought God would have done something by now!"

Here is a secret: If we believe the promise because we know God is faithful, then it doesn't matter whether it takes 10 minutes or 10 years. God is *still faithful*. It may be hard to remain steadfast in faith as we see time passing, but if we allow delay to bring discouragement, then we are in trouble. Part of our trouble, as twenty-first-century Christians, is that we go through life with a vending-machine mentality. We want everything right

GOD'S PICTURE OF ANSWERED PRAYER IS NOT A VENDING MACHINE BUT A HARVEST.

now! We do this with God, too. We need a breakthrough from heaven, so we go to the divine vending machine, slip some faith in the slot, push the prayer button and look for the answer to pop out. If the answer is not there in two minutes, we're ready to start kicking the machine. That's *not* how prayer works!

God's picture of answered prayer is not a vending machine but a harvest. We have a need, so we sow our faith in the good soil of God's promise. As we sow, we nurture and water our promise until the time of harvest. When the time of harvest has fully come, we reap based upon what we have sown!

Signs of Hope Deferred

Hope deferred occurs when weariness brings wavering. We enter hope deferred when the tiredness of pressing on makes us want to give up. Here are some signs that we have succumbed to hope deferred.

We know we are on shaky ground when we no longer want to hear God's promise. As we go through testing, God will give us prophetic words to encourage us and keep us focused on His promise. When Abraham was waiting for a son, God repeatedly came to him and said, "I'm going to give you a son!" (see Gen. 15:4; 17:19; 18:10). God repeats His Word to us to strengthen our faith. We can *know* we are in hope deferred when we hear God's promise and want to explode. It is not a good sign when we say, "I am tired of hearing that promise! I don't want any more prophetic words! I just want it to happen."

A second indication of hope deferred is when Satan is able to plant a thought in our mind, such as *I can't take any more of this!* If we find that phrase repeatedly coming into our mind, we can be sure that the thought is from Satan. God would not tell us that! God has promised that He will *not* test us beyond what we are able to take (see 1 Cor. 10:13). Our problem is that sometimes God knows we can handle more that we think we can handle—or want to handle. When we hear that discouraging thought in our mind, we need to confront it and say, "That is a lie, Satan, because God will *not* give me more than I can handle!" Then we need to lift up our shield of faith and declare God's Word: "I can do all things through Christ who strengthens me!"

If Satan begins to plant thoughts of weakness and defeat in our mind and we choose to *agree* with him, we have put down our shield of faith. We must realize that we *can* be disqualified. A great example of someone who put down his shield of faith is Moses. Yes, Moses was a man of great faith. There was hardly anyone in the Bible with more faith than Moses. In God's Hall of Fame for people of faith in Hebrews 11, Moses got five verses! Of all of the men of faith in the Old Testament, Abraham is the only one with more verses of praise than Moses.

Moses was a man of persevering faith. He was in the wilderness for 40 years by himself. Then he led Israel out of Egypt and was in the wilderness for another 40 years. He had a faith that persevered. The only problem is *Moses didn't persevere quite long enough!*

Moses fell into the trap of hope deferred. He eventually grew weary of the battle. As Moses was in the wilderness with all the people around him moaning, complaining and accusing, he began to grow weary. He took his eyes off God and put them on his situation.

At one point the Lord said to Moses, "Because you did not believe Me, . . . you shall not bring this assembly into the land which I have given them" (Num. 20:12). To understand the significance of this penalty, we need to understand that it was Moses' call and destiny to bring the people *out* of Egypt and *into* the Promised Land. That was what Moses had been created to do—it was his purpose in life!

Moses had gone through years of preparation in Egypt and more years of preparation in the wilderness. By Moses' hand, God performed miracles to release Israel from slavery. Then Moses led the people through the Red Sea and down to Sinai, where he gave them God's Law. Moses led the people to the border of the land, and when the people sinned, he led them through the wilderness for 40 more years. But the goal was always to take them into the Promised Land.

Moses almost made it, but he stopped too soon! He resorted to his human way of looking at things. Faith comes by hearing, but remember we can hear God's voice and Satan's voice. Moses went back to what he had heard earlier in his life instead of hearing the truth God was speaking to him that day. If we do not stay in faith, we can miss the promise.

TESTING AND PERSEVERANCE

Many people give up too soon. I have seen many people with incredible giftings and anointings come into the Church over the years. Some have incredible prophetic words over their lives. They want to serve God, and they want to minister—but they want it all right now! Some seem to have the attitude, *Lord, I want to serve You. Which spotlight do You want me to stand under?*

God usually has us put these people through a time of testing. He will say, "Try them in a place of humble service first and see how they do." So we put them in a place of humble service, and for a few months they do very well. But when promotion does not come as soon as they anticipated, they give up and wander around in the wilderness for a while. Some assume their gifting was unappreciated, and they leave the church. Others sit in rejection for months and then come back and try again.

One couple went through this process two or three times. They were two of the most talented people I have ever met, and they had a real call from God to lead worship. But they would not be faithful to their commitments for more than a few months. When they got discouraged, they would stop showing up for worship practice. I finally told them, "If you would just stay steady for six months, you would make it!"

God says we must complete the testing before we can obtain the promise. James wrote, "Blessed is the man who perseveres under trial, because when he has stood the test, he will receive the crown of life that God has promised" (Jas. 1:12, *NIV*). We do not obtain the promise without passing the test.

Steps to the Next Level
There is a *process* to get to the *promise*. When God sees that we are

capable of moving into the next level of His promise, His first step is to put testing in our life.

Paul had to go through this testing. From the time God called Paul until He sent him out on his first missionary journey was 16 years! Paul waited 16 years for God to open the door to his destiny. These were 16 years of learning, preparation and testing. Because Paul remained faithful and passed the test, God was able to send him out as an apostle to change an empire.

None of us enjoys waiting, but the promise is worth the persevering.

Obtaining the promise is like running in a race. We are racing down the track, giving it all we have. Our chest is heaving and our muscles aching. We are growing more weary with each step. We don't think we have the strength to go on. But then we come around the last bend, and we see the finish line. Somehow we reach down inside and find resources we did not think we had. We get a second wind and sprint down the track to win the race.

> SOME PEOPLE DON'T SEE GOD WORK BECAUSE GOD NEVER PROMISED THEM WHAT THEY ARE TRYING TO GET.

When we go through a time of testing, it will take longer and be harder than we thought, because God's goal is to bring forth endurance. His goal is to bring us to a new level, to make us stretch further and reach higher than we thought we could. It is only then that we discover that as we persevere, we inherit the promises.

Secrets of Persevering

Winning the race and reaching the Promised Land sounds so good, but how do we survive the trek? How do we pass God's tests? Here are some guidelines that work.

Be sure we are on the right path. Some people don't see God work because God never promised them what they are trying to get. If we feel like we are not getting anywhere, we need to step back and make sure we have heard God. We should go to leaders whom we trust, who know us. We need to listen—and take notes—as they speak into our life. We need to ask them, "Is this really what God is saying to me?" If it isn't God's promise, no amount of perseverance will get us there. Presumption is not faith. We need to be certain that we have heard from God.

Know that God won't test us beyond our ability. If God puts us in a situation in which we need a certain level of strength, it's because He knows that it is available to us. God puts us in a difficult testing after He has looked at us and said, "I believe this person can make it through this test and into the blessing." When we see the difficulty of the test, we should realize that *God believes in us.* God would not give us the test if He did not believe we could make it through.

Develop a reflex of thanksgiving. When we are being tested, we need to develop a reflex action. Just like Pavlov's puppies developed the reflex to automatically respond every time they heard a bell ring, we need to develop an automatic response to calamity, namely, the reflex of thanksgiving. When the big test comes and our faith is stretched to the breaking point, this reflex will see us through. When unexpected calamity strikes and we want to throw down our shield and give up, the thanksgiving reflex will keep us from going under!

Here's how it works: Whenever a circumstance rises up against us, the first three words out of our mouth need to be

"Thank You, Lord!" We just got a bad report from the doctor, an unexpected bill or a letter from the lawyer; what do we say? "Thank You, Lord!" The Word says we should give thanks in every circumstance (see 1 Thess. 5:18). We can act upon this verse and ask God to build that reflex into us. We can thank God in every situation and receive the strength to keep our shield of faith in place.

Remember that discouragement does not come from God. When we feel that mantle of discouragement coming down over us, we should not just sit there and wallow in it! We need to rise up in faith and say, "This isn't from God! God doesn't want me under this!"

Keep going no matter what. Over the years, I've learned that if we press on with God, we do win. The only thing that will cause us to lose during a time of testing is stopping. If we keep moving, God will make a way and we will win.

James 1:4 (*NASB*) exhorts us, "Let endurance have its perfect result, that you may be perfect and complete, lacking in nothing." This is God's goal for our life. He wants us to "be perfect and complete, lacking in nothing."

Righteous like an Oak Tree

Someone once said, "When God wants to grow a squash, He takes six months. When God wants to grow an oak tree, He takes a hundred years." Isaiah tells us that God is building us into "oaks of righteousness, the planting of the LORD, that He may be glorified" (61:3, *NASB*). God could do a rush job and get it done in six months, but all we'd be is a squash. God has not destined us to be a squash. He has called us to be an oak tree. *Don't despise the waiting. Remember that the promise is worth the persevering!*

TESTING AND PROPHETIC FULFILLMENT

In *The Best Is Yet Ahead*, Rebecca Sytsema and I wrote about the test of Abraham. Our shield is linked to Abraham's faith because we have been grafted into Abraham's covenant. The blessings we receive from God today were initiated through His relationship and covenant agreement with Abraham.

In order to help us more fully understand how prophetic fulfillment works from generation to generation, let's take a look at Abraham and see the six steps it took to pass the covenant promises onto Isaac so that Isaac could come into his prophetic fulfillment.

1. A persevering faith

Abraham had a covenant promise for his family, which included a son being born to him from his aging wife, Sarah. Abraham had to stand and believe God for His promise as the years of natural fertility dwindled and passed. Even so he maintained a persevering faith, and the promise through which the covenant would be passed was finally born when Isaac arrived.

As we have said before, God has a destiny for every bloodline and we need to come into agreement with what God is trying to do, even if we don't know the specifics of how it will work out. It requires a persevering faith that often overlooks the natural circumstances in favor of *But God*! As we allow that faith to arise within us, we will see the covenant promises of God over ourselves and our families begin to take shape as God causes the circumstances of our lives to come into alignment with His promise to us. We see other individuals in the Bible that are great examples for us concerning persevering faith. Daniel withstood the lions, Caleb in his 80s advanced into his promise, Sarah in her 90s conceived. What wonderful examples of faith.

2. The covenant promise will always be tested

In Genesis 22 we see that Abraham underwent a strong test. Here God calls Abraham to take his precious son, Isaac, and lay him on an altar in sacrifice. It must have taken a tremendous level of obedience on Abraham's part to make that choice and lay his son down to die. But Abraham understood that this was God's directive. He knew that somewhere in the midst of his obedience to God, God would have to settle the outcome and fulfill His covenant. The obedience was up to Abraham, and the rest was God's problem. Of course we know that in the end Abraham was not required to follow through and kill Isaac, but even if he had, God would have had to find another way to fulfill His covenant.

The testing of our promises is an inevitable step in prophetic fulfillment. In fact, if we don't get past that step, our promises will not be fulfilled, either for ourselves or for our families. Like Abraham, we need to understand that our role is obedience to God, and the rest is up to Him. Period.

3. Testing unveils provision

Once Abraham passed the test, provision came. There in a thicket was a ram caught by its horns. Abraham was able to take the ram and offer it as a sacrifice to the Lord instead of offering Isaac. In fact, Abraham named that place "The LORD Will Provide" (Gen. 22:14) as a testimony to God supplying what was needed. As we pass the testing of our promises, God will reveal hidden provision for moving us forward. Things that we were not able to see before will become evident to us, and we will gain new strategy for continuing to move toward God's plan for us.

4. Promises extend to new generations

Another result of Abraham passing the test was that God extended a new promise to him for the generations of his family to come. God said to him, "By Myself I have sworn, says the LORD, because you have done this thing, and have not withheld your son, your only son—blessing I will bless you, and multiplying I will multiply your descendants as the stars of the heaven and as the sand which is on the seashore; and your descendants shall possess the gate of their enemies. In your seed all the nations of the earth shall be blessed, because you have obeyed My voice" (Gen. 22:16-18).

God is always looking for how to connect His promises from one generation to another generation. We must acknowledge the generations and see that God has promises for the generations to come. Even those prodigals who seem so far from God's plan for their lives always have some opportunity to return to God's plan for them.

5. Connecting to pass the mantle

Many times we must participate in supernatural connecting so the next generation receives the blessing from the previous generation and continues progressing in that blessing. Years later, Abraham had come to an awakening that the promise that he had been given, which had been extended to Isaac, could not be completed if Isaac had no wife with whom he could have children of his own. Abraham, therefore, instructed his servant to find just the right wife for Isaac. Through Abraham's careful instructions, the servant found Rebekah, who became Isaac's wife.

What is it that we are to provide the next generation for them to move on in God's covenant promise for them? Certainly a godly upbringing (Proverbs 22:6 says, "Train up a child in the way he should go, and when he is old he will not depart from it."), an understanding of who they are in Christ, and lots of prayer top the list. But beyond good parenting, we need to gain instruction from the Lord regarding our role in assisting the next generation reach prophetic fulfillment in their lives.

6. Conception for the future

Isaac gaining a wife was not enough to ensure that God's promise would carry on. He and

Rebekah had to conceive the next generation. There has to be a conception in order to bring forth the prophetic fulfillment. We must not stop until we are sure that we have conceived and brought to birth all that God asks of us.

God's covenant promise to Abraham also required obedience for prophetic fulfillment. Abraham was required to go through all these steps and partner with God in faith and obedience, even in the face of years of discouragement. Yet through Abraham's faithfulness, all the families of the earth truly have been blessed. What is it that God longs to accomplish through your family line, and what role do you play in your family's prophetic fulfillment?[4]

THE FINAL SCORE: A TESTIMONY

By withstanding the test, Abraham secured a testimony that was passed from one generation to another. "Testimony" literally means "witness."[5] A testimony is a declaration or statement made to establish a fact. Abraham's testimony becomes an affirmation, evidence and proof of the delivering power and character of a holy God. That testimony still speaks today. Revelation 12:10-11 reads:

Then I heard a loud voice saying in heaven, "Now salvation, and strength, and the kingdom of our God, and the power of His Christ have come, for the accuser of our brethren, who accused them before our God day and night, has been cast down. And they overcame him by the blood of the Lamb and by the word of their testimony, and they did not love their lives to the death."

When we go through testing, the enemy wants us to fail and lose the favor of God. However, every time we pass a test, our faith increases and a testimony is established. The testimony is what Satan hates. Therefore, during our test he does everything to weaken us and destroy our testimony.

A test is a refining examination by trial to prove the value or ascertain the nature of something, or an event or set of circumstances that proves or tries a person's quality of character. When we triumph in our trial, a declaration is established. This profession, or public avowal, of faith overcomes the enemy. It proves the reality of God and His covenant. A testimony is the proof of our faith in action. Our shield of faith shines when our testimony is proclaimed.

Giving testimony is a function of the spirit of man. The Ark of the Covenant held the Ten Commandments, or Testament of God. The Ark had to be carried in front of the people and advance first before the people of God could fully enter into the Promised Land. Our testimony is a proclamation of a strengthened spirit that declares the goodness of God. It overcomes the enemy and gives us the confidence for us to advance into the future.

Notes

1. Chuck D. Pierce and Rebecca Wagner Sytsema, *Possessing Your Inheritance* (Ventura, CA: Renew Books, 1999), pp. 66-67.
2. Ibid., pp. 67-68.
3. Chuck D. Pierce and Rebecca Wagner Sytsema, *The Best Is Yet Ahead* (Colorado Springs, CO: Wagner Publications, 2001), pp. 67-68.
4. Ibid., pp. 81-84.
5. *Merriam-Webster's Collegiate Dictionary*, 10th ed., s.v. "testimony."

CHAPTER 7

BURSTING PAST BLOCKADES

When the Lord called Jeremiah, He showed the prophet that He had set him over kingdoms and nations, and his ministry would go through phases. He would root out, pull down, destroy and throw down. Many Christians have been tearing down and rooting out long enough. Just as the Lord told Jeremiah that he would build and plant, now it is time for us to do the same! Building for the future and planting to bring forth increase sometimes are more difficult than tearing down and rooting out.

When God extended the call, Jeremiah's mind and emotions could not grasp the magnitude of God's grace. He actually tried to explain to God why he would not be capable of doing what God was asking him to do. So many times we do the same thing. We try to convince God that He really doesn't know what He is doing when He asks us to move forward into a new dimension that we are unsure of. When He tells us it's time to leave our comfort zone, we explain to Him why we really shouldn't move. Thank God He does not always listen to us when we disagree with His plan. In so many words, He told Jeremiah, "Don't tell Me you are too young, not mature enough to do this that I'm asking you to do" (see 1:7). We embrace God's call by faith.

God was determined to tear down what was contrary to His covenant plan for Israel, so He could rebuild them into a new, sharp threshing instrument (see Isa. 41:15). He used Jeremiah as a prophet in this tearing-down process, and then He started releasing His plan to rebuild Israel for the future. We find this recorded in the books of the restorative prophets Haggai and Zechariah. Throughout the building process, the enemy discouraged the Israelites, so they would stop building. God then had to use another prophetic voice to get them to start building again. He even gave them a promise that "the glory of this latter house shall be greater than of the former" (Hag. 2:9, *KJV*), if they could only get it built.

GOD IS POURING OUT UPON HIS PEOPLE A MIND FOR INCREASING HIS KINGDOM.

Many times the enemy attempts to block God's building plan for our life and the vision He has released to us. I feel this applies to each one of us personally. This also applies to our businesses and even the corporate vision that we are aligned with in ministry. So many times we know we are to move forward, but we encounter resistance that blocks our way.

God is pouring out upon His people a mind for increasing His kingdom. We, therefore, need to allow Him to give us His mind to build. When Nehemiah was rebuilding the wall, he said the people had a mind to work, a mind to build what God wanted built (see Neh. 4:1). The mentality that we have for building and for seeing harvest upon Earth is very important. If our mind is not connected to the mind of Christ to build His house on Earth, we won't see God's will come to fruition for what He wants accomplished in our generation.

THE MIND NEEDS TO BE BUILT FOR INCREASE

In *The Future War of the Church,* Rebecca Sytsema and I wrote:

In order to tap into God's mind for building, it is important to have a biblical understanding of increase. When we look at increase in the Word of God we see that it is linked with government. Isaiah 9:7 reads, "Of the increase of His government and peace there will be no end." Increase is also a harvest principle. Increase rises through faith, and follows effort and deeds linked with faith. Increase comes through connecting with one another. There is a need for us to link together and gain strength in multiple and corporate measure as opposed to independence. Increase is also a reward for obedience. There is joy in obedience, and joy causes our strength to increase. And from strength we are capable of building God's strategic plan for the future. These are days when God is building His house. To build means to add to and establish. The Hebrew word actually signifies the adding of sons and daughters so that the plan of God can be passed from one generation to another.[1]

The mind of increase is a mind of faith.

THE ENEMY DEVISES BLOCKADES

In almost every example of building in the Bible, there is also a strategy of the enemy to stop the building process of God's covenant people. His covenant people are part of His covenant plan, and for His plan to be seen in the earth we must build. Faith builds! Faith looks at a demolished building and sees it rebuilt. Faith looks at a wall with many breaches and gaps and sees it totally intact. Faith sees a dilapidated house and sees it fully restored. Faith sees the redemptive plan in a war-torn nation. Faith sees a vibrant church and house of prayer for every cultural group. Faith sees past the enemy's blockades. Faith sees—and faith builds!

Faith Overcomes the Enemy's Blockades

In the book of Haggai, we find that the people began building and then stopped building. They grew disinterested! They became discouraged! And they even became disillusioned with God's restorative plan! Then they began the task of rebuilding the Temple in Jerusalem. However, they were stopped after opposition mounted against this plan—both externally and internally. The issue here is that even though God had a building plan, the enemy tried to block the plan. Only faith can overcome the enemy's blockades. As I've studied this subject, I felt the Lord has given me 12 key principles to help us sidestep the enemy when we feel blocked:

1. *We should desire to worship God in a new way.* Worship is an expression of faith! In Exodus 14, we see that God intervenes for the people to enable them to move forward. He had given them a covenant promise 400 years earlier. Each one of us, as God's son or daughter, also has a covenant promise. Through our cries during difficult circumstances, He sends a deliverer to lead us forth into our promise. Sometimes we have to fight for our promise. We need to declare that we will be released from everything that is hindering us from worshiping God in a new way. Let's break out of old worship patterns!

2. *We need to exercise whatever authority God has given us.* We all know this familiar story: Once the people of Israel were released, they got to a place where the sea was before them and the enemy was behind them. Even though they were confused and didn't understand how to proceed, Moses said to them, "Do not be afraid. Stand still, and see the salvation of the LORD, which He will accomplish for you today. For the Egyptians whom you see today, you shall see again no more forever" (Exod. 14:13). There comes a time when God wants to rid us of the enemies of our past. The Lord told Moses, "Tell the children of Israel to *go forward*" (v. 15, emphasis added). Many times when we, like Moses, feel blocked, we want to stop. Then He told Moses, "Lift up your rod" (v. 16)— Moses' symbol of authority. We have a measure of authority that God has given us. If we exercise that measure, our way will begin to open up. The Lord will overtake our enemies so that we can proceed into our next phase of victory. We cannot look back at our

enemies. This is a time to remain one step ahead!

3. *We must express faith by praising God.* Praise causes our dry times to end, refreshment to come and our path to open up. In Numbers 20, Edom refused passage to Moses and the people of Israel. Even though Moses negotiated with Edom twice, Moses did not receive favor for the people to pass through on the way to the promise. Sometimes that happens to us. We do everything we know to try to convince an adversary to allow us safe passage, and yet we don't seem to make any headway. We find in Numbers 21 that the people got to another place where they didn't seem able to move forward, and they grew very thirsty without water. We too will have dry times along the path to our promise. God commanded the people to gather and sing. Verse 17 informs us that they began to sing, "Spring up, O well," the well began to fill with water so that they could drink and be refreshed. When we stop and praise, we will advance. Corporate worship is necessary for our victories in the days ahead. We need to find our place of corporate worship. Even if we don't feel like worshiping, we need to worship. God will refresh us; He will give us strength; and we will be able to advance.

4. *We do not need to fear addressing old issues that have never been dealt with fully.* Many times we want to have faith to move into our future, but there is something in our past that we need to have faith to address. In 2 Samuel 5, David came into the anointing promised many years before. His first assignment was to overthrow the Jebusites at Jerusalem. David knew he had to establish a place for God's presence. The Jebusites

should have been overthrown when Joshua and the people had crossed into the Promised Land 400 years prior to this. They were a people descended of Canaan (who had been cursed by Noah). For David to become captain and ruler and to enter into what he had been anointed to do, he had to overcome the Jebusites. Many times an old iniquitous pattern, or path, in our life resurfaces. We can never enter into all of the benefits of God's redemptive plan for our life until this iniquity is overturned. The time for victory is now!

5. *We are compelled to allow the Lord to reveal unconventional ways to overtake our enemies.* Faith is not afraid to go into sewage. In 2 Samuel 5, David stood back and saw an entryway into Jerusalem. However, it was through sewage! If we look carefully, God will show us the entryway into our victory. We need to take a deep breath and go through our sewage phase. Jerusalem was David's place to establish God's presence. This would be where the Ark would eventually rest. If we are willing to go through our sewage, we will only stink for a short period. Then God's presence will be established in us and His sweet-smelling favor will surround us.

6. *We must watch for the enemy's backlash.* Once the Philistines heard of David's anointing, they came to stop him from advancing. The enemy detests when we move forward, and He abhors the thought of the anointing of God increasing in us. The Philistines attacked David, yet God gave David victory. However, once David had victory, the enemy actually regrouped to come against David again. Faith keeps

your mind, heart and spirit active and discerning the enemy's plans.

7. *We can be creative in confronting the enemy.* Faith is creative. We must never presume upon God and think that we can confront the enemy in the same manner

WE CAN BE CREATIVE IN CONFRONTING THE ENEMY.

we confronted him in our last season of victory. When the Philistines regrouped against David, he asked the Lord, "Should I go up again?" The Lord said, "Yes, but not in the same way." The Lord told David to listen for the sound of the wind in the mulberry trees (see 2 Sam. 5:23-24). We need to allow the Holy Sprit to supernaturally fill us. We must listen for the voice of the Holy Spirit. There is a sound from heaven that will guide us. The Spirit of God in us will cause us to hear that sound. Listen for the new sound!

8. *When we seem blocked, we need to quickly seek the Lord and wait for His revelation.* In 2 Chronicles 20, we learn about a confederation of enemy forces coming against Jehoshaphat. Even though fear gripped him, Jehoshaphat fasted and sought the Lord, which caused the Lord to move upon the prophet Jahaziel. Jahaziel began to prophesy God's strategy for victory. We must listen for the prophetic word. The prophetic word will lead us into success and victory—it is one

of our most effective weapons against the enemy. Faith cometh by hearing!

9. *We should take the time to write down the enemy's threats and then present the situation to the Lord.* So many times when the enemy is coming against us, we try to go to everyone around us who will listen to our problems. However, we need to present our case to the Lord. In 2 Kings 18–19, we find that Sennacherib, a type of enemy of God's covenant, overtook everyone in his path. This ruler then threatened to overcome Hezekiah. Many times the enemy draws our eyes to what he is doing, and then he convinces us that we are next in line. Sennacherib sent a letter to Hezekiah. Hezekiah presented this letter to the Lord as a prophetic act. When we write down the enemy's threats and hold them up to the Lord, He will give us an order, a strategy and assistance. Faith overcomes!

10. *We must not let an atmosphere of unbelief prevent us from speaking out in faith.* In Luke 4:1-14, Jesus had entered into the wilderness and gained victory over the enemy. He then returned from the wilderness with power. However, when He went to Nazareth and declared who He was and that He was anointed to bring forth God's plan in the earthly realm, the atmosphere of unbelief attempted to stop Him from moving forward in His Father's purpose. In the midst of an atmosphere of unbelief, we must speak faith.

11. *We need to learn when to change direction.* Jesus sidestepped the enemy many times. Many times the religious enemy of that day would rise up to stop Jesus from moving forward. According to John 8:59 and 10:39, Jesus moved out of the enemy's path. He hid

Himself and escaped the hand of the enemy who was attempting to seize Him. If Jesus could make it to His destination, the cross, Jesus in us can bring us to our destination. We should let Jesus reveal the path through any blocked circumstances.

12. *We can expect God to move on our behalf.* In Acts 12:1-4, Herod imprisoned Peter (a lot of the Early Church leaders were persecuted). The Church began to pray for Peter. Then an earthquake occurred. (We should watch for natural circumstances to work for our benefit, too.) However, when Peter showed up at a house church, the people could not believe it was Peter. When we pray, we should expect God to move!

Even though the enemy tries to block us from advancing toward all that God has for us, we cannot submit to a blocked path. We must submit to God and resist the devil. He will flee and we will advance.

Faith Overthrows the Enemy's Decrees

I awakened one morning hearing these words:

There is an intense period of prayer and fasting coming to the Body. This period will be your shifting time for the season of revival that is now upon you. This will be a period of removal. This will be a period of restoration. This will be a period of preparing the way and setting the course for the future. This will be a time to go through narrow, confining places in your life. By pressing through the confining places I will begin to define your future. I will remove weakness, infirmity and that which has bent you over and kept you from advancing in the past. This will open the door for spiritual *breakthrough*. This is a door that has been sealed tight. Do not fear the intensity of this time in your life, but receive My strengthening. I will remove religious spirits that are stopping My kingdom from advancing. For now is the time for the generation that is rising to be released with a new mantle. This will be a time to define the mantle of authority to be worn by the carriers of vision into the next generation. This is a time for your enemies to be fully defined and to develop a strategy for their exposure and overthrow.

These sentiments remind me of Esther—an Old Testament book that I love. Esther is filled with demonstrations of faith that build up my faith. Now is a time to pray, read and live out this book. God is raising up new Mordecais and Esthers (the primary

GOD IS RAISING UP NEW MORDECAIS AND ESTHERS TO INFLUENCE THE WORLD IN THE DAYS AHEAD.

characters whose stories of faith are told in Esther) to influence the world in the days ahead. These individuals will do radical exploits in God's name.

During the time of Esther, the enemy had entered in through the gates of the city and was planning to undercut the covenant blessings that God had for His people. Mordecai exposed the enemy's plan and took his authority at the gate (see Esther 6:12). Centuries later Jesus enunciated the God-given principle behind this and other similar acts of faith: "I also say to you that you are Peter, and on this rock I will build My church, and the gates of Hades shall not prevail against it" (Matt. 16:18). We too can grab hold of this promise and apply it to our life. This is not a time for hell to prevail at our gate.

The gate of a city was where all business transactions and legal matters occurred. The city gate was also the place where entrance into the city was permitted or forbidden. A biblical gatekeeper was one who guarded access to a city (see 2 Sam. 18:26; 2 Kings 7:10-11), a residence (see John 18:17), the sacred precincts of the Ark (see 1 Chron. 15:23-24) or the Temple (see 1 Chron. 23:5). Temple gatekeepers were charged with preventing anyone unclean from entering the Temple (see 2 Chron. 23:19) and with guarding the Temple treasuries and storehouses (see 1 Chron. 9:26; 26:20-22; Neh. 12:25). Mordecai was a good gatekeeper. He knew the enemy had a plot. He had overheard the plan and linked it with Haman who wanted to annihilate God's covenant people in the land. Haman had prepared a noose for God's covenant people (see Esther 9:25). Esther shows us how to see the destiny of God's covenant manifest itself when we legislate authority at the gates, as Mordecai did (the enemy will always attempt to plot, or utter decrees, against us).

Mordecai knew he had to have a connection to prevent the enemy's plan from prevailing. Esther was his connection; she had been positioned by God for "such a time as this" (Esther 4:14). Many Christians today are being similarly positioned to see the plan of the enemy. Others are being positioned to be the connecting point to overthrow the enemy. I am praying that any plot of the enemy to try and stop the covenant blessings of our inheritance from coming forth would be revealed. We must find the divine connections and overthrow the enemy's plan! This is the time to overthrow decrees that have been set against God's covenant people and that keep us from corporately advancing.

Esther prayed and fasted three days prior to setting the wheels in motion to overthrow the enemy's plan. She had faith to go into the king's court, because she had spiritually prepared herself by fasting for three days. Fasting helps prepare us for what we must face in our battle ahead. Esther was at the right place at the right time and did the right thing. Therefore, she had victory over the enemy.

HELP IS ON THE WAY

The cry of help is a cry of faith. So many times I've had to cry out for the Lord to come to my aid. In times of distress, I usually read the psalms.

> May the LORD answer you in the day of trouble, may the name of the God of Jacob defend you [or set you high above your enemies]; may He send you *help* from the sanctuary, and strengthen you out of Zion. May He grant you according to your heart's *desire*, and fulfill all your purpose. Now I know that the LORD saves His anointed (Ps. 20:1-2,4,6, emphasis added).

This was a typical psalm prayed by the congregation at a time of giving and sacrifice just before going to war. It is a prayer of faith and declaration. By praying this psalm, we know God has heard us, so now we can move forward into His plan of victory against our enemies.

> I called on the LORD in distress; the LORD answered me and set me in a broad place. The LORD is on my side; I will not fear. What can man do to me? The LORD is for

me among those who help me; therefore I shall see my desire on those who hate me. It is better to trust in the LORD than to put confidence in man. It is better to trust in the LORD than to put confidence in princes (Ps. 118:5-9).

"Distress" means the seizure or detention of one's goods or resources, a state of danger or desperation, to become worried or traumatized, or a pain or suffering that buffets the body. Distress is also associated with coming to a narrow place and having to endure the pain in that narrow place in order to come into the new. Distress is also related to the word "travail." In our distress, when we call unto the Lord, the Lord comes. Again, faith cometh by hearing! When we are in the narrow place, the Lord begins to release revelation that shows us how to break through.

I got up one morning to go preach, and I asked the Lord what He was saying to the congregation where I was ministering. I felt an impression with these words: "Tell them that help is on the way. I AM the Helper. If they will call out for Me, I will help them." I began to preach and make faith declarations from this word. While I was preaching, I felt the Spirit of God impress me to tell the people to write down the three areas that they needed help with, and that we were not to have an altar call. If they would write down their three areas of need and give their list to the elders, they would be contacted that week and begin to see breakthrough. God's miracle-working gift of faith began to take hold in that congregation. Below is one of the many testimonies of what began to happen.

A Pond Can Help!
Sharon Roberts writes the following:

On November, 26, 2000, I was in a church service where Chuck prophesied: "I AM entering you into a new day of deliverance and I say from this new day of deliverance I will break open new realms of spoils that have been held up." This was a word that I had pondered in my heart.

However, in April 2002, I was laid off from my job. I was out of work for five months exactly. During this time I considered selling my property. I love living in the country and I love my animals, but without a job it cost too much to keep up. At church one day Chuck prophesied to me, "Whoa! Stay put! Stay put! God is going to use you for the building program." I wondered, *How did you know I was considering moving?* I wondered, *What building program and how will He use me?* I put aside the idea of selling my place. I stayed put. When I became employed in September of that same year, I gave my first week's check to our church as a first fruits offering. I expected that my barns would be filled with plenty and my presses would burst forth with new wine. I just didn't know how it would come to pass. But God knew. I believe the following events are just the beginning, because God is a God of seed time and harvest. It's a law He set into motion, and it will exist as long as the earth remains.

I live out in the country on about 22 acres of land. Drilling companies are drilling natural gas wells all around my property. I did not want one drilled on my land because of the destruction and so on. I don't own the mineral rights. I prayed, "Please, God, I don't want them to drill on my property." I went to church that morning and heard Prophet Chuck Pierce speak on "Help Is on the Way."

A man working for one of the companies called me one afternoon and asked me if I had seen the surveying stake they had put on my land marking the next well. I told him there was none on my land. He said he was coming out to look because it should be there. I was out feeding my animals when he drove up. We saw that the stake was on the property just south of my border. While we were talking, he mentioned that they needed water to drill. My pond was very close. He asked if I would sell them water out of my pond. He said they would pay between $3,000 and $4,000 for it. I told him, "Yes." A few weeks later a man knocked on my door. He said they would pay me $2,000 for the pond water. I told him what the other man had said, but he would not change his price. I finally told him I wanted $2,200 at least. He said he'd see what he could do. They set up the pump that night, before I got paid. I felt foolish that I had nothing in writing and they were already using my water. I kept waiting and waiting for the money, but it did not come. I decided to tithe on it (just to give the devil a black eye), so I put $220 extra in the offering the next Sunday. By Wednesday I had the check for $2,200. I communicated with the first man about the difference in the sums of money. About two weeks later he called me to tell me he had a check for the difference between $2,200 and $3,500 (which is what he thought was a fair amount). Included in the check was $3,500 more for water for the next well they wanted to drill—$7,000 for the two wells. I praised God and it entered my mind that I should now make a first fruits offering rather than tithe. I told the Lord that I would do this if that is what should be done. I still considered it a one-time occurrence, so I did not know if first fruits applied, but I was willing. A couple of weeks later the first well man called to tell me that they needed more water than my pond contained. He asked if I would let them drill a water well on my land and use the water to "fracture" three to five more wells. He said they would pay me $3,500 for each. When he brought me a contract and a check for the first three wells to be fractured, I noticed that it said $4,500 for each well to be fractured. The man said he had made a mistake when he said $3,500. In less than six weeks, God blessed me with $20,500 in a manner that I could never have imagined. I believe that more will follow. The well man said that they may drill as many as five or six other wells, depending on how well the present ones produce, and if they do, they will use my water well to fracture each of them at $4,500. Help truly came! God used an unexpected resource that I had to bring great help, so I could keep my farm.[2]

Perhaps each of us has a pond or some other unexpected resource that God can use to provide for us.

The Holy Spirit Is Our Helper

To really understand faith and enter into the faith dynamic for this hour, we've got to know the Holy Spirit. The Holy Spirit is that mysterious third Person of the Trinity whom the Father moves through. The Holy Spirit inhabits our human spirit and connects us to the heavenly abiding place that God has prepared for us. He is the Person who reveals the will of God. The Holy Spirit is the One who empowers us to accomplish the will of God and to become a son or daughter of God. The Holy

BURSTING PAST BLOCKADES 121

Spirit discloses the personal presence of God and His Son, Jesus Christ of Nazareth, to us.

The Holy Spirit manifests Himself to us and inhabits us. He makes us all that the Father intended us to be in the earthly realm. The Holy Spirit is our Helper. Thus, when we cry out for help, we are crying out for a manifestation of His presence. The Holy Spirit is the Spirit of truth. Therefore, He reveals truth to us. And when we worship in spirit and in truth, we enter into the reality of the Lord Jesus Christ.

"Help" is to exchange or lay hold of a necessary support. It also means to render assistance, especially to one in a needy condition. There are several aspects of help that I feel we need to understand:

1. Help is a shout that causes someone to run to our benefit. This is supernatural grace in a timely fashion (see Heb. 4:16).
2. Help can be an aid rendered to us by an ally (see Acts 26:22).
3. Help comes when someone partakes in our need and renders support (see 1 Tim. 6:2).
4. The Holy Spirit will help us in our time of need by taking hold of our spirit and praying through us when we don't know how to pray (see Rom. 8:26).
5. We can render help when we aid anybody (see Matt. 15:25; Mark 9:22-24).
6. The word "help" is linked with joining together and serving someone so that their mission gets accomplished (see 2 Cor. 1:11).
7. We can cooperate and work alongside others in a synergistic fashion so that strength is multiplied (see 1 Cor. 16:16).

We must not quench the Holy Spirit, for when we quench the Holy Spirit, we quench our helper. When we grieve the Holy Spirit, our helper is grieved and we do not have the strength to accomplish what we need to accomplish. Cry out for help and let help come! Psalm 46:1-3 reads:

> God is our refuge and strength, a very present help in trouble. Therefore we will not fear, even though the earth be removed, and though the mountains be carried into the midst of the sea; though its waters roar and be troubled, though the mountains shake with its swelling.

He is there. Cry out!

The Holy Spirit is the person that dwells within us that causes our faith to manifest itself. The gifts of God work through the manifestation of the Holy Spirit. This manifestation is linked with our shield of faith. When we need a word of knowledge or a word of wisdom, the Holy Spirit brings it to us. From this manifestation, the faith we need comes through this word of knowledge or wisdom, which causes our shield to be flexible enough to quench any fiery dart that the enemy sends. The gifts of prophecy, faith, tongues, interpretation of tongues, discerning of spirits, healing and miracles are all manifestations of the Holy Spirit, which cause our shield of faith to function properly.

FAITH AND AUTHORITY UNLOCK OUR DESTINIES

One of my favorite stories and probably the most important illustration of the concept of faith is found in Matthew 8:5-13—the story of the centurion. This man comes to Capernaum to find Jesus and plead with Him concerning his servant who is dreadfully tormented and paralyzed. Because of this man's cry for help, Jesus said,

> "I will come and heal him." The centurion answered and said, "Lord, I am not worthy that You should come under my roof. But only speak a word, and my servant will be healed. For I also am a man under authority, having soldiers under me. And I say to this one, 'Go,' and he goes; and to another, 'Come,' and he comes; and to my servant, 'Do this,' and he does it" (vv. 7-9).

Jesus marveled at this man's faith. Matter of fact, He called it great faith and exclaimed that He had not seen this type of faith in all of Israel (see v. 10). He then said to the centurion, "Go your way; and as you have believed, so let it be done for you" (v. 13). The centurion's servant was healed that same hour (see v. 14).

One of the greatest lessons of faith is the relationship between faith and authority. My father died prematurely when I was 16. Even though I lived through some traumatic times, I was never left fatherless. God placed fathers and mothers in my life so that I would never be outside an authority structure. I believe this has been a key to my personal development of faith. Faith not only works vertically (between us and God), but it also works horizontally—in the way that we steward the relationships of those whom we have authority over. The understanding of authority is a key to unlock our destiny and enter into God's promises by faith.

THE REVELATION AND THE CONFESSION OF FAITH RELEASE KEYS

In Matthew 16:19, we find the phrase "keys of the kingdom." This phrase related to the authority delegated to Simon Peter to "bind" and "loose." This authority given to Peter and the apostles cannot be separated from the heavenly insight and confession that Jesus is the Christ, the Son of God. It was the revelation given to and confessed by Peter that called forth our Lord's blessing. The confession of our faith activates our authority. Confession means we are in harmony with and saying what the Father is saying in heaven. Peter's authority as an apostle was based upon his divinely given confession. The authority to bind and loose—the result of receiving "the keys of the kingdom"—is a stewardship, a delegated authority from Christ (compare Matt. 16:19 to John 20:21-23 and Rev. 1:18; 3:7-8).

I travel much through the world ministering to God's people, declaring Kingdom breakthrough and harvest release—by "harvest release" I mean that Jesus releases people who are captive to sin and He wants us to participate with Him in releasing people today. When in Rome, Italy, a mission team that I was leading spent a day praying at various sites that the Holy Spirit led us to. One of the places we visited was the Mamertine Prison, where it is believed Peter (and perhaps Paul also) was held prisoner in Rome. A strong presence of the Lord filled the place. We recalled the great cloud of witnesses who had gone before us, not loving their lives even unto death. We declared that the true apostolic leadership God is raising up today would be willing to defend the faith—whether chained and bound in a pit or whether free. As we exited the Mamertine Prison, we saw statues of Peter and Paul: Peter was holding keys and Paul had a sword. We declared that no longer would the keys of the Kingdom be held out of the Body's reach but that we would receive authority to unlock revelation and spiritual harvest.

There is so much we can learn from Peter. One of the most powerful prophecies of our Lord is found in Matthew 16. This is where the Father reveals Himself to Peter, and Peter recognizes that Jesus is Christ, the Son of the living God. Jesus then prophecies:

> Blessed are you, Simon Bar-Jonah, for flesh and blood has not revealed this to you, but My Father who is in heaven. And I also say to you that you are Peter, and on this rock I will build My church, and the gates of Hades shall not prevail against it. And I will give you the keys of the kingdom of heaven, and whatever you bind on earth will be bound in heaven, and whatever you loose on earth will be loosed in heaven (vv. 17-19).

This particular prophecy is part of the DNA of every blood-bought believer of Jesus Christ. When we receive divine revelation and make a confession of our faith in the Person of Jesus Christ, God activates the building plan that He designed for our life.

I am praying for the readers of this book:

1. That the Spirit of revelation rest upon you and that you recognize the Lord in your midst!
2. That you review how you are building God's plan for your life!
3. That you look at the vision that you are a part of to see your place in the building process!
4. That hell and the power of death do not stop you from advancing in the building plan that you are a part of!
5. That you resist the gates that are preventing you from moving forward and shouting victory.
6. That you gain the keys that you need to advance. A key denotes authority and unlocks!

7. That you see into heaven and bind and loose so that
   the world around you reflects what heaven is declaring!

BINDING AND LOOSING RESULTS FROM THE CONFESSION OF FAITH

In that cold, underground chamber in Rome, which was only accessible by climbing down a rope through a hole, we gave thanks for what the apostles had written and shared about how to be free in Jesus Christ. We then declared that the Church would not fear what is ahead but choose to remain free in the Lord at all costs. That's my prayer for us also. Our confession released apostolic authority in the earth and gave the power of binding and loosing (see Matt. 16:19; 18:18)—a phrase used to describe the work of scribes by which they exercised through teaching and judging. The scribes also could exclude persons from the community (see Matt. 18:15-17), but Christ denounced them for misusing their key of knowledge (see Luke 11:52). They also blocked the entrance to the Kingdom (see Matt. 23:13). In their place, through the gift of the Spirit, the disciples received the authority to proclaim forgiveness and judgment (see John 20:23).

The confession of faith has the power to bind and loose. When we confess our faith, we receive keys to unlock God's kingdom purposes of our life and to forbid unwanted entry of the enemy. Jesus says, "I will give you the keys and you will be able to forbid and you will be able to permit" (see Matt. 16:19). Revelation and authority are linked together. This is an hour when God is saying to us that He is ready to give us keys. These keys will unlock the supply of faith and God's power we need to advance His Kingdom covenant purposes. These keys will forbid hindrance to His purposes, causing His will in heaven to be released on Earth.

At the time that Jesus gave these keys to Peter, the scribes of that day had the authority to study the Scriptures and then communicate to the people what was in the Scriptures. Jesus knew, however, that the scribes were not really communicating His building plan to the people. What Jesus was really saying was that He was going to take the keys from the scribes and hand them over to the disciples, making them the future leaders of His Church; and he was also going to give them authority to forbid or permit, based on the revelation of His authority.

We know that Jesus eventually made His disciples into apostles; and they went forward, not only unlocking the kingdom of God throughout the region, but also building His house in that day and season after God gave them the necessary wealth. We find this principle in Acts 4:32-37. This was the beginning of the early harvest that occurred after the ascension of the Lord Jesus Christ. That harvest has continued throughout the generations. In some generations, it has been more plentiful than others. However, we are about to see that harvest accelerate, and we will need to have a mind for increase in the Kingdom if we are to be a part of that acceleration.

The keys to the Kingdom given to Peter were also a symbol to describe the locking or unlocking sins, and they illustrate his authority in binding or loosing (see Matt. 16:19). In verse 18, the same power was given to the apostles and the Church as a whole; it was not an exclusive gift given to any one person or church. The question of how sins are forgiven is raised in the meaning of binding and loosing. Whatever the Church declared to be wrong or right would have been anticipated and ratified in heaven by divine sanction. This means that whosoever shall have been forgiven on Earth shall have been forgiven in heaven. Heaven sets the standard, and Earth follows heaven's lead. It is the responsibility of believers to have a forgiving spirit and to teach the conditions of forgiveness (see Matt. 6:12). John 20:23 (*KJV*) quotes Jesus as saying:

> Whosoever sins ye remit, they are remitted unto them; and whosoever sins ye retain, they are retained.

This means that the Church is to proclaim the way of salvation; those who accept Him are forgiven, but those who reject Him are condemned. Binding or loosing of sins is determined by the hearer's response to the gospel. Of course, the power to loose sins comes ultimately from the blood of Jesus (see Rev. 1:5).

IT IS TIME FOR BREAKTHROUGH!

One of the names and characteristics of God is the breaker. The Lord is ready to establish Himself at the gates of our life, church, city and nation. Micah 2:13 reads: "The one who breaks open will come up before them; they will break out, pass through the gate, and go out by it; their king will pass before them, with the LORD at their head." Barbara Yoder says in *The Breaker Anointing*:

> This Breaker has all authority to enter into every other kingdom and nation and begin to break us out of those kingdoms' rule into a place of freedom and liberty, life and inheritance. He not only breaks us out of the imprisoning kingdom but also establishes a new Kingdom in its stead. He is *the* King of kings.[3]

Elijah travailed with his head between his knees until the cloud that he saw by the Spirit in the heavens came into the earthly realm (see 1 Kings 18:36-38). "Breakthrough" is a term that means an offensive thrust that penetrates and carries beyond a defensive line in warfare; a sudden advance in knowledge or technique; moving through an obstruction; to disrupt the continuity or flow of an old system, bring it to an end, and begin something new.

We must raise our shield of faith!
It is time for the Lord to break through,
the Church to break out
and the enemy's plans to break up!

Notes

1. Chuck D. Pierce and Rebecca Wagner Sytsema, *The Future War of the Church* (Ventura, CA: Renew Books, 2001), p. 158.
2. Sharon Roberts, personal communication to Chuck Pierce, n.d.
3. Barbara Yoder, *The Breaker Anointing* (Colorado Springs, CO: Wagner Publications, 2001), p. 39.

CHAPTER 8

THE WHOLE ARMOR OF GOD

When we make the choice to be single-minded, yielded to God and true worshipers of Him, He becomes our shield of faith. In the Word of God, we see many verses that declare the Lord as our shield. We can compile some of them to get a clear picture of God's promise to us (see Gen. 15:1; Deut. 33:29; 2 Sam. 22:3,36; Ps. 5:12). Filling in our name where indicated, we should repeat the following as often as needed to prepare us for battle.

I AM here to shield you today. Do not be afraid,
[your name]; I AM your shield, your very great
reward. Blessed are you, [your name]! I AM your
shield and helper and glorious sword. Your enemies

*will cower before you and you will trample down their high
places. I AM God your rock. [your name], take refuge in
my shield and the horn of My salvation. I am your stronghold, your refuge and your Savior from violent men. I have
given [your name] My shield of victory. I have stooped
down to make you great. I bless the righteous; therefore,
I will surround [your name] with favor as with a shield.*

Isn't that an incredible promise? God declares that He is our
shield! Not only is He our shield, but also our faith and trust in
Him become our shield to quench all of the enemy's fiery darts.

UNDERSTANDING THE SHIELD

Let's look again at what the shield actually represents. The shield
is illustrative of God's protection, His truth and His salvation.
However, the shield only becomes active when we respond in
faith. The ancient soldier's chief defense, his shield, was made in

THE SHIELD IS ILLUSTRATIVE OF GOD'S PROTECTION, HIS TRUTH AND HIS SALVATION.

various forms and of various materials. The shield in a siege covered the soldier's whole person, and at the top, it had a curved
point or a square projection with the body of the shield—like a
roof at right angles. This was to defend the combatants against
missiles thrown from walls.

"Shield" is the rendering of the first three of the following
Hebrew words, of which the first two are the most frequent and

important. The fourth word is not literally translated as "shield" but is similar.

1. *Sinna*. This shield was used for protection and was large enough to cover the whole body (see Pss. 5:12; 91:4). When an army was not engaged in conflict, the sinna were carried by the shield bearer (see 1 Sam. 17:7,41). Generally, the word is used with "spear" as a formula for weapons (see 1 Chron. 12:24; 2 Chron. 11:12).

2. *Magen*. This shield was smaller, a buckler or target, probably for hand-to-hand combat. The difference in size between this and the above-mentioned shield is evident from 1 Kings 10:16-17 and 2 Chronicles 9:15-16, which describe that twice as much gold was used for the latter as for the former. This shield is usually coupled with light weapons, such as the bow (see 2 Chron. 14:8) and darts (see 2 Chron. 32:5, *KJV*).

3. *Shelet*. The form of this shield is not well known. Some translate "shelet" as "quiver," others as "weapons." However, when we compare 2 Kings 11:10 with 2 Samuel 8:7, 1 Chronicles 18:7-8 and 2 Chronicles 23:9, it becomes evident that it simply means shield.

4. *Sohera*. This means "buckler" and is found only in Psalm 91:4 (*KJV*), where it is used poetically.

We also have the Greek word thureos (see Eph. 6:16), a large oblong or square shield.

The sinna was the shield of the heavily armed soldiers (see 1 Chron. 12:24). Goliath was also protected by a sinna—in his case a man carried the shield in front of him as he entered battle (see 1 Sam. 17:7,41). Bowmen carried the magen (see 2 Chron. 14:8).[1]

The New Unger's Bible Dictionary and *Fausset's Bible Dictionary* provide detailed information about shields and other weapons. According to both dictionaries the ordinary shields used by the Hebrews were oblong or square wooden frames that were covered with leather and could be burned easily (see Ezek. 39:9). Some shields were covered with brass or copper, and when the sun shone upon them, they turned red (see Nahum 2:3). The soldiers rubbed their shields with oil which made the leather smooth and slippery (see 2 Sam. 1:21-22; Isa. 21:5). Oil also kept the metal from rusting. Putting oil on a shield served another purpose as well. "Anoint the shield!" (Isa. 21:5), Isaiah warned Babylonian revelers as they prepared to defend themselves. In Psalm 47:9, "the shields of the earth belong to God." These shields are the princes who act as protectors of their people (see Hos. 4:18). Except during actual conflict, the shield was kept covered (see Isa. 22:6). Most golden shields (see 1 Macc. 6:39, *TJB*) were probably only gilt. The shields used by the generals of Hadadezer (see 2 Sam. 8:7) and those made by Solomon (see 1 Kings 10:16-17; 14:26) were ornamental pieces of massive gold, as were the shields later sent to Rome as gifts (see 1 Macc. 14:24; 15:18, *TJB*). Bronze shields also were used but only by leaders and royal guards (see 1 Sam. 17:6; 1 Kings 14:27).[2]

Faith is our shield "above all" (Eph. 6:16); in other words, it is the last item we put on and covers everything else we wear. However, Sinaiticus and Vaticanus manuscripts read "in all things." Faith will certainly "quench all the fire-tipped darts of the evil one" (see 1 Pet. 5:9; 1 John 5:4,18). Fire-tipped darts were canes. Soldiers would ignite the tips and propel them toward the enemy.[3]

DEVELOPING AND INCREASING THE SHIELD OF FAITH

In an online article, Bible teacher Rick Joyner asked, "Is your faith prominent?" He then wrote the following:

> If a soldier is marching toward you with his shield held rightly, it will almost certainly be the most prominent thing you see about him. If it is clean and shined up, it will be even more so. Could that be said of us? When others look at you, is your faith that prominent? Our shield of faith is also what extinguishes any arrow the enemy flings at us. If we are constantly getting hurt and wounded, it is almost certainly because we are not carrying our faith right. Faith is basically seeing Jesus and knowing where He sits above all rule, authority, and power. If we know this, then it is impossible for the enemy to get a shot in while the Lord is not looking. Therefore, all of the trials that come our way are for a purpose—our maturity. We should therefore embrace the trials as opportunities. In this way, each trial the enemy flings at us will actually cause our faith to grow so that it becomes even more difficult for him to wound us.[4]

Our faith must always be visible and constant, but we also need to be flexible with our faith. Joyner continues:

> A skillful warrior in biblical times used his shield effectively regardless of which direction the attack was coming. A warrior who rigidly walked with his shield in one place would become an easy target for someone who shot at him from an unexpected direction. We, too, must learn

to be flexible with our faith. There is faith for salvation, and faith for healing. There is faith for authority over demons, and there is faith to bring in God's provision. There is faith for our children, churches, and cities, and faith for our country to see God move in them. So if our faith is going to be useful for these, we must see them with trust in God and anticipation of His victory, and not look at them in doubt, regardless of what problems arise. The key is to keep our shields up, regardless of what disappointments may come. There are times when things will happen with all of these that could be very disappointing. However, to become disappointed is to drop our shield of faith. When arrows start coming, it is not the time to drop our shields, but to raise them up with even more resolve. The arrows will come, which should never discourage us, but cause us to grip our faith even tighter, and hold it up with even greater vigilance.[5]

PUTTING ON THE ARMOR

Weapons of war are used both offensively and defensively. Since warfare is mentioned so frequently in the Bible, so are arms and armor. Knowledge is key; therefore, it's very important that we have knowledge of the armor that God has given us. The forms and uses of weapons and armor evolve from the beginning of the Old Testament period until the end of the New Testament period. Certain weapons that were common in one period became outdated and fell out of use in later times.[6]

The comprehensive Hebrew term for defensive and offensive weapons is *kelee* (see Gen. 27:3; 1 Sam. 17:54; Deut. 1:41); in Greek, *hoplon* (see 2 Cor. 10:4) is the word for weapons of war. Other Greek words refer to armor-bearers and armories. The sons of light had to be equipped to deal with the sons of darkness. Various items of armor have great spiritual significance:

> For He put on righteousness as a breastplate, and a helmet of salvation on His head; He put on the garments of vengeance for clothing, and was clad with zeal as a cloak (Isa. 59:17).

In Ephesians 4:22-24, Paul instructs the people of Ephesus to "put off, concerning your former conduct, the old man which grows corrupt according to the deceitful lusts, and be renewed in the spirit of your mind, and that you put on the new man which was created according to God, in true righteousness and holiness." In other words, we are to remove our old lifestyle of disobedience and enter into a lifestyle of obedience from our newly created identity, which was given to us when Jesus came to live in our heart and we received the Holy Spirit. Obedience is linked with faith, so we actually put on faith.

Paul instructs the people of Ephesus to receive a spirit of revelation and wisdom. He tells them to be rooted and grounded in love. He encourages them to walk in unity. He explains God's government, which has been released to equip them in the

HELL CANNOT WITHSTAND THE UNITY OF FAITH OF BELIEVERS.

earthly realm and to bring them into a unity of faith. Once we put on faith and activate our faith, we unite our faith with that of other believers. This produces a unity of faith. Hell cannot withstand the unity of faith of believers. Paul then tells the people of Ephesus not to grieve the Holy Spirit, because the Holy Spirit empowers them to maintain their new lifestyle. He also tells them to walk in love and wisdom. Once he has explained the proper authority relationships, he then tells them to get clothed so that they can withstand the enemy, the devil, who will try to rob them of their destiny:

> Finally, my brethren, be strong in the Lord and in the power of His might. Put on the whole armor of God, that you may be able to stand against the wiles of the devil. For we do not wrestle against flesh and blood, but against principalities, against powers, against the rulers of the darkness of this age, against spiritual hosts of wickedness in the heavenly places. Therefore take up the whole armor of God, that you may be able to withstand in the evil day, and having done all, to stand.
>
> Stand therefore, having girded your waist with truth, having put on the breastplate of righteousness, and having shod your feet with the preparation of the gospel of peace; above all, taking the shield of faith with which you will be able to quench *all* the fiery darts of the wicked one. And take the helmet of salvation, and the sword of the Spirit, which is the word of God; praying always with all prayer and supplication in the Spirit, being watchful to this end with all perseverance and supplication for all the saints (Eph. 6:10-18, emphasis added).

DEFINING ALL THE PIECES

Notice that according to Ephesians 6:11, we must put on the whole armor. We have described the shield, but the shield alone will not provide the protection we need for victory. The shield is only one part of our defensive armor, which also includes a helmet and a breastplate.

The helmet secures our thoughts and protects our mind. We must capture each thought and bring it under the obedience of Christ.

The breastplate was a piece of elaborate embroidery about nine inches square and worn by the high priest upon his breast as he ministered in the Tabernacle or Temple. It was set with 12 stones with the name of 1 of the 12 tribes of Israel engraved on each stone. Made like a purse, the breastplate was constructed of gold metal; blue, purple and scarlet yarn; and fine linen. It was securely tied to the ephod. Inside the breastplate were two unknown stones—the Urim and Thummim—worn over the heart (see Lev. 8:8). The breastplate was called the breastplate of judgment, because these stones were the means of making decisions (see Exod. 28:2,15,28-30). The purpose of the breastplate was (1) to show the glory and beauty of the Lord (see v. 2); (2) to be a continuing memorial before the Lord (see v. 29); and (3) to be a means of making decisions (see v. 30).

Then there were offensive weapons, of which the sword is the most frequently mentioned in the Bible. The earliest swords in the ancient world were usually straight and double-edged, akin to daggers, and used for stabbing (see Heb. 4:12). In the time of the Egyptian new kingdom, the longer-bladed sword began to be used widely. With the arrival of the sea peoples, the long straight sword began to enjoy popularity. It usually was carried in a sheath, suspended from a belt (see 2 Sam. 20:8). To judge from the various artifacts found in Egypt and Mesopotamia, hilts were often ornamented. The sword is used as a symbol for the Word of God (see Ezek. 21:9; Eph. 6:17).

Remember that faith comes by hearing—hearing by the Word of God. When we engage in offensive action, the sword and shield must be used together. We will never be consistent in our faith without developing the discipline of studying to "show thyself approved" (2 Tim. 2:15, *KJV*).

WE ARE TO GIRD OURSELVES WITH TRUTH. THIS WEAPON IS THAT WHICH IS RELIABLE AND CAN BE TRUSTED.

We are to gird ourselves with truth. This weapon is that which is reliable and can be trusted. The Bible uses truth in the general factual sense. Truth may designate the actual fact over appearance, pretense or assertion. In Zechariah 8:16 (*NRSV*), the Lord of hosts declared:

> These are the things that you shall do: Speak the truth to one another, render in your gates judgments that are true and make for peace.

When Jesus asked, "Who touched My clothes?" (Mark 5:30), the woman who had been healed through touching Jesus' garments "fell down before him, and told him the whole truth" (v. 33). In 1 Timothy and 2 Timothy, truth is correct knowledge or doctrine. Certain individuals had departed from proper doctrine. Some "forbid marriage and demand abstinence from foods, which God created to be received with thanksgiving by those who believe and know the truth" (1 Tim. 4:3, *NRSV*). Others "swerved from the truth by claiming that the resurrection has already taken place" (2 Tim. 2:18, *NRSV*).

Another key piece of the armor is our feet—figuratively we are to wear peace on them like we would wear Birkenstocks. Peace is not simply a weapon—it is better understood as a sense of well-being and fulfillment that comes from God and is dependent on God's presence. As we activate our faith, ascend in worship and come boldly before the Lord in the Throne Room, not only does our shield become powerful enough to quench the fiery darts of hell, but we also begin to have total confidence to move forward. Once we have peace on our feet and in our arsenal, we can walk forward on the path that God has set before us.

The concept of spiritual peace is most often represented by the Hebrew root *slm* and its derivatives—the most familiar being the noun *shalom*. It basically means wholeness, or well-being. We find the Lord manifesting Himself to Gideon as *Jehovah Shalom* (see Judg. 6:23-24). God gave Gideon peace to move forward against his enemies. Peace is a gift from God, for only God can give perfect peace (see Ps. 4:8; Prov. 3:17; Ezek. 34:25). When we accept Christ as our Savior, we obtain spiritual peace. By trusting God and loving His law, peace comes (see Ps. 119:65). Peace is also linked with our relationship with the Lord. When we lift up and live by the truth, we encounter peace (see Esther 9:30 for an illustration of this concept). When we have a good relationship with God and the people He has put in our path, we can experience spiritual peace.[7]

God is "the God of peace" (Rom. 15:33; Phil. 4:9; 1 Thess. 5:23; Heb. 13:20). The gospel is the good news of peace (see Acts 10:36; Eph. 6:15), because it announces the reconciliation of believers to God and to one another (see Eph. 2:12-18). God has made this peace a reality through Jesus Christ, who is our peace. We are justified through Him (see Rom. 5:1), reconciled through the blood He shed on the cross (see Col. 1:20) and made one in Him (see Eph. 2:14). In Him we discover the only One who can give absolute peace (see John 14:27). This peace manifests itself as an inner spiritual resolve by each of us (see Rom. 15:13; Phil. 4:7; Col. 3:15). It is associated with how we receive God's salvation (see Matt. 10:13), freedom from distress and fear (see John 14:27; 16:33), security (see 1 Thess. 5:9-10), "mercy" (Gal. 6:16; 1 Tim. 1:2), "joy" (Rom. 14:17; 15:13), "grace" (Phil. 1:2; Rev. 1:4), "love" (2 Cor. 13:11; Jude 2), "life" (Rom. 8:6) and "righteousness" (Rom. 14:17; Heb. 12:11; Jas. 3:18). Such peace is a fruit of the Spirit (see Gal. 5:22) and it forms part of "the whole armor of God" (Eph. 6:11,13). This peace equips us to withstand the attacks of the enemy.[8]

Notes

1. *International Standard Bible Encyclopaedia*, electronic database. PC Study Bible V3.3A for Windows, Copyright © 1988-2002, © 1996 by Biblesoft, s.v. "armor."
2. *The New Unger's Bible Dictionary* (Chicago: Moody Press, 1988) on Biblesoft software (Seattle, WA) and *Fausset's Bible Dictionary,* electronic database on Biblesoft software.
3. Ibid.
4. Rick Joyner, "Developing and Growing Your Shield of Faith," *Elijah List— Prophetic Words and Prophecies*, June 27, 2003. http://www.elijahlist.com/ elijahlist.htm (accessed July 2003).
5. Ibid.
6. *Nelson's Illustrated Bible Dictionary* (Nashville, TN: Thomas Nelson Publishers, 1986).
7. Ibid., Hulitt Gloer, s.v. "arms" and "armor of the Bible."
8. Ibid.

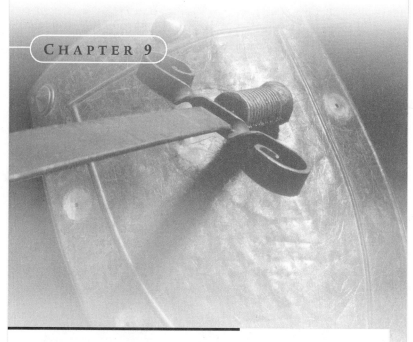

CHAPTER 9

FROM WEAKNESS TO PERFECTION

According to Romans 1:17, we go from "faith to faith." Romans 10:17 (*KJV*) puts the concept this way: "faith cometh." These verses tell us our faith is not stagnant and should be increasing from one level to the next. The disciples asked the Lord to increase their faith (see Luke 17:5). I like what Barbara Wentroble says when she ministers: "If I have the same level of faith this year that I had last year, I've backslidden."[1] Faith should be ever increasing, maturing and coming into a manifestation of why God released the faith to us in the first place.

RECOGNIZING OUR BIG GOD

Wendell Smith, a wonderful pastor in Seattle, describes how faith can grow, as evidenced by the 10 levels of faith found in the Scriptures.

Our faith should increase from the level we are at today to a new level of trust in God. As the apostle Peter described it, we should "grow in the grace and knowledge of our Lord and Savior Jesus Christ" (2 Peter 3:18). There are ten levels of faith listed in the Scriptures:

1. **Weak Faith**—the word means "to be feeble and without strength, powerless, needy, or sick." This is the beginning of faith for most (see Romans 4:19; 14:1).

2. **Lacking Faith**—Paul prayed for the Thessalonians that what was lacking in their faith might be proved for them. The Greek word points toward a deficiency of resources; poverty, lack, or destitution (see 1 Thessalonians 3:10).

3. **Little Faith**—this word carries the meaning of "trusting too little." We have moved from infancy, but are still toddlers in our faith. If we still struggle with doubt, we are at the level of little faith (see Matthew 16:8; 14:31).

4. **Seed Faith**—at this level, faith can now produce something. The word used here for seed means "grain," such as a seed of wheat or corn. This seed is powerful and holds the

potential of a full-grown plant or tree (see Matthew 17:20).

5. **Increasing Faith**—we now enter the levels of faith where growth is evident. This word literally means "to cause to grow or to increase," and it is used of plants, infants, multitudes of people, or of personal Christian growth. We are only half way there and must keep growing (see 2 Corinthians 10:15).

6. **Exceedingly Growing Faith**—Paul commended the Thessalonians for their growing faith. He uses a word in the Greek language that means to "grow beyond measure." It is the same word as level five, but with the Greek prefix *huper*. We would use the word "hyper," meaning something super, extra, or special. Now we are really growing in our faith (see 2 Thessalonians 1:3).

7. **Rich Faith**—an incredibly descriptive word meaning, "abounding in resources, abundantly supplied, or abounding in virtues and possessions." This level of faith abounds in the wealth of the kingdom of God (see James 2:5).

8. **Strong Faith**—Abraham had this kind of faith. The word means to be "endued with strength." Now we are graduating to a level of faith that has endurance in its mix. This is where faith becomes invincible (see Romans 4:20).

9. **Great Faith**—there were only two people in the Scriptures who were commended for great

faith. They were both foreigners to the nation of Israel, one a Roman centurion and the other a Syro-Phoenician woman. They both impressed Jesus with their resilient faith on behalf of another. Great faith is usually mobilized on behalf of others. There are two definitions of great faith. The Greek word used in reference to the Roman centurion described faith of "great quantity." In regards to the amazing woman whose daughter was delivered from a demon, a much stronger Greek word is transliterated, mega, meaning "greatest in intensity, extent, stature, rank, authority, and power; of great importance or excellence" (see Luke 7:9; Matthew 8:10; 15:28).

10. **Perfect Faith**—the Apostle James describes perfect faith as belonging to one who is a doer of the word and exercises faith to change. It means to "complete something or to carry through thoroughly; to bring to an end; accomplish and fulfill." It is not enough to just confess faith. The definitive test is the doing and performing of it, demonstrating faith in real life situations. This is faith that is tested, perfected, and matured. This is our ultimate goal (see James 2:22).

We can grow from weak faith to strong faith, from little faith to great faith, from lacking faith to rich faith, and from seed faith to perfect faith in the process of fulfilling the incredible destiny that the Lord has planned for our lives.[2]

The point is that our faith should never remain static. We should be moving from weak to perfected faith. Perfected faith means we have come into a place where we've completed a cycle in our life, and what needed to be accomplished has been accomplished. We trusted and we saw. To have our faith grow to complete maturity is akin to a torn net that was mended. We can view our shield of faith as having holes in it and needing restoration. Once our net is mended, or our faith is complete, we can begin to draw in and harvest the promise for which we have been trusting.

GOING UP TO A NEW DIMENSION

Our desire must be to enter into a new dimension of faith. If we have weak faith, we must desire that it become strong. And the only way that is going to happen is by our "going up" in worship and entering a new place of faith. Let's explore this principle of going up.

I minister quite often with Pastor Dutch Sheets, author of *Intercessory Prayer* and *Watchman Prayer*. When we minister, we talk about going up through the door of heaven and boldly entering into the Throne Room where glory faith dwells. Dutch combines the following five verses in Ephesians to express God's purpose of ascending into a new dimension of faith. Read and meditate on the following:

> Blessed be the God and Father of our Lord Jesus Christ,
> who has blessed us with every spiritual blessing in the
> heavenly places in Christ, which He worked in Christ
> when He raised Him from the dead and seated Him at
> His right hand in the heavenly places, and raised us up
> together, and made us sit together in the heavenly places

in Christ Jesus, to the intent that now the manifold wisdom of God might be made known by the church to the principalities and powers in the heavenly places, for we do not wrestle against flesh and blood, but against principalities, against powers, against the rulers of the darkness of this age, against spiritual hosts of wickedness in the heavenly places (Eph. 1:3,20; 2:6; 3:10; 6:12).

I believe these verses summarize the Lord's call to us at this time—to go up, ascend, and war from a heavenly perspective!

MANY OF US NEVER EXPERIENCE A NEW DIMENSION OF FAITH BECAUSE WE DO NOT GO UP IN WORSHIP.

Many of us never experience a new dimension of faith because we do not go up in worship. In *The Worship Warrior*, John Dickson and I wrote about how we can follow Jesus by ascending in Jesus until a heavenly portal opens and faith pours out on us. I will explain this concept in greater detail later in this chapter; but first I want to illustrate this going up in worship:

When I was working in downtown Houston, some days I would ride the bus to and from my home in the north part of the city. I had gotten up one morning and worshiped from 5 A.M to 6 A.M. and was overwhelmed by the presence of God. I then got ready and caught the bus at 7 A.M. On the way, I began to read the book of

Ephesians. I had just started when I got to Ephesians 1:3-6:

> Blessed be the God and Father of our Lord Jesus Christ, who has blessed us with every spiritual blessing in the heavenly places in Christ, just as He chose us in Him before the foundation of the world, that we should be holy and without blame before Him in love, having predestined us to adoption as sons by Jesus Christ to Himself, according to the good pleasure of His will, to the praise of the glory of His grace, by which He made us accepted in the Beloved.

I began to praise and thank the Lord for choosing me before the foundation of Earth. The heavens opened. I could see all the future blessings that God had for me. I could also see the blessings that were there for the generations before me that were never taken and the blessings that the Lord had for my children to come. Suddenly the Lord began to pour faith into my spirit—it was as if a funnel extended from heaven right into the bus.

I could not contain myself, so I shouted, "Hallelujah!" Those people around me looked startled. I thought to myself, *Surely they can see and feel what I see and feel.* I said, "Lord, I am so filled with faith, I do not know what to do." He said to me, "Give it away to one of those sitting around you." I asked a lady who was sitting in front of me if she had a need and if I could pray for her. She began to share her problems. I knew then what it meant to pray the prayer of faith.[3]

Choosing Submission over Resistance

Worship is a choice. Our will must be activated in worship. Faith is also a choice. Our will must be active for us to enter into a new dimension of faith. Faith is an action! The action of faith is linked to how our mind and will interact with the Spirit of God who dwells in our human spirit. The will many times does not want to become active and submit to the Spirit of God. When

Our will must be active for us to enter into a new dimension of faith.

the will resists submission our faith suffers. James 4:7 instructs us, "Submit to God. Resist the devil and he will flee from you." This is how our shield of faith when used properly overcomes the enemy's fiery darts. We submit our will and choose to worship God.

One morning I heard these words from the book of James deep in my heart: in the valley of decision. I knew if I was to make the right decision, the decision that God would have me make, I was going to have to allow my will to be yielded to the power of the Holy Spirit. Then I would be able to make the best choice God had for my life. As I researched this "valley of decision" in Joel 3:14, I found that this was the *valley of Jehoshaphat*. Jehoshaphat had made reforms that changed the course of his nation, but then he had to meet his greatest external threat. An alliance was coming against him and he faced insurmountable odds. In the midst of this great trial, his first step was to humble himself. Three elements of spiritual discipline put God's covenant people in a right position for victory: (1) fasting, (2) prayer, and (3) praise. With these spiritual dynamics working, prophecy and revelation could be released so that in this valley they would emerge victorious. Their battle was a battle of faith! God's battle was to dismantle and remove the enemy by dispatching the hosts of heaven. We find the covenant people subdued their enemy by faith through praise and worship.

Shechem, the place of choice, has always been important throughout biblical and Church history. We are at Shechem, the place of choice, in Church history! This is causing us to choose God's covenant purposes in the earth. What the Church chooses will determine how the conflict of the nations will be resolved. How the Church makes this choice will establish the release of the Lord's inheritance on Earth for this generation. Many times we reflect what is happening in the Church corporately in the choices we make in our personal lives. Today's choices in relationships, positions (both territorial as well as vocational), resource facilitation, provision, supply and ministry alignments determine our future. In Joshua 24:14-15, at the end of Joshua's time of leadership, he admonished the people to

> put away the gods which your fathers served on the other
> side of the River. . . . Serve the LORD! And if it seems evil
> to you to serve the LORD, choose for yourselves this day
> whom you will serve, whether the gods which your
> fathers served . . . or the gods of the Amorites, in whose
> land you dwell. But as for me and my house, we will serve
> the LORD.

Let's look at Shechem for a moment. It was located between Mount Ebal and Mount Gerizim, offering a large, natural amphitheater for a gathering of all the tribes. In Joshua 8:30-35, we see that this place was the spiritually significant, defining place of meeting for the Israelists before they went in to fully possess the land. The invincible place of Jericho had been overcome, and the mistake at Ai had been rectified. Then Joshua worshiped and renewed God's covenant with Israel. He read all the words of the Law—the blessings and the cursings. The people gathered in this beautiful valley and heard the words shouted like a antiphon from one mountain to the other. They heard the message perfectly; they were not confused about what they heard.

The first step in making our choice so that our faith increases is to stop and worship God. We must exalt Him for our key victories and thank Him for His grace even in your past mistakes. As we present ourselves without reserve to God and empty ourselves before Him, we will clearly hear the choice He has before us without confusion. Confusion is always linked with a spirit of Babylon (where the devil had erected a structure filled with deception). The Lord will bring our heart and mind to a place of peace. Peace means wholeness. Faith and peace work together.

There are three generations now standing at Shechem! They are listening carefully to the choice that is before them. This day is filled with blessings or cursings! The blood of our Savior can deliver us from the curse and cause us to enter into the eternal blessings in heavenly places (see Eph. 1:3). However, we must look through the confusion of Babylon to make the correct choice at this time. When we hear the choice of our blessing, God writes the boundaries of that choice upon our heart. The power of His Spirit allows us to move freely by grace within those boundaries. If we will make His presence our focus in life, the voice of blessing will become louder than the voice of cursing. If we choose blessing, then the events of the world will line up with the choice of God's people. The Lord is opening His treasure in heaven based upon this choice that we His people are making. We must activate our will now and align it with God's so that the confusion that is occurring in the world will not cause us to shake but will cause us to stand steady in the midst of the war ahead. Then we can watch the next generation receive the benefits and results of our choice.

WAFFLING BETWEEN TWO OPINIONS

The Bible warns us about double-mindedness, a huge enemy of faith:

> If any of you lacks wisdom, let him ask of God, who gives to all liberally and without reproach, and it will be given to him. But let him ask in faith, with no doubting, for he who doubts is like a wave of the sea driven and tossed by the wind. For let not that man suppose that he will receive anything from the Lord; he is a double-minded man, unstable in all his ways (Jas. 1:5-8).

When we commune with God and ask for wisdom, we are promised it will be given to us. Wisdom overcomes and dismantles our enemy. However, if we are double-minded and doubting, the enemy mocks, ridicules and reminds us of our unworthiness. As a result, we waver between two opinions. Doubting becomes a way of life. The Bible helps us stir clear of this predicament by defining the roles of our soul and our spirit. We get in trouble when our soulish nature rises up and we begin to have a conflict within ourselves. We have misgivings. We waver in our decision making. We get caught between hope and fear. When our spirit prevails, we refocus on God and obtain single-mindedness, peace and victory.

On Mount Carmel, Elijah was in a contest with the prophets of Baal. This contest was held to determine who was Lord of the region. The people were double-minded. Through circumstances, God had brought them to a place of choice. They kept waffling between worship of God and worship of an idol. God defied all human reasoning at this point. It was Elijah against the 450 prophets of Baal—impossible odds in the natural—yet nothing was impossible with the Lord. The people needed to "get unhalted!" "Halt" means to walk with a limp or become lame; to stand in doubt between two courses or paths; to display weakness or imperfection; to put things on hold; to cease marching or journeying; or to discontinue or terminate a project for lack of funds. On Mount Carmel, worship became the turning point. Elijah built an altar in the name of the Lord and allowed the river of God to flow. Then the fire from heaven fell. This caused the people to see that "the LORD, He is God!" (1 Kings 18:39).

By faith we must choose to confront and worship in the midst of our enemies. Our faith choice demonstrates God's power instead of just a form of godliness.

We must make a choice today to increase your faith.

Notes

1. Barbara Wentroble (Wentroble Christian Ministries Apostolic Prophetic Conference, Dallas, TX, February 7, 2003).
2. Wendell Smith, *Great Faith: Making God Big* (Portland, OR: City Bible Publishing, 2001), pp. 88-89. Used by permission.
3. Chuck D. Pierce and John Dickson, *The Worship Warrior* (Ventura, CA: Regal Books, 2002), p. 131.

CHAPTER 10

MOVING INTO A NEW DIMENSION

I want to share a biblical pattern that will help us come to a new level of faith. Over the years, I have come to understand that there are *levels* of faith, each with a *dimension* of revelation. John Dickson and I shared these in my book *The Worship Warrior*.[1] They are vital for us to understand our study.

SEVEN DIMENSIONS OF FAITH

To fully establish our shield of faith and press through all the opposition of the enemy, we need to allow God to bring us through these seven dimensions into the fullness of His glory. As we look at each dimension let's ask God to bring us to a new level of faith.

1. Historical Faith

When we have this type of faith we apprehend and ascend based upon historical accounts of how God has worked throughout time. We read a fact from history, and it causes faith to rise up.

A good example of this is the revival that occurred in Wales at the beginning of the twentieth century. The Welsh revival was one of the most well-documented moves of the Spirit in history. Newspapers tracked the progress of the revival as it moved from county to county. The presence of God would be manifested in a given city, and the entire city would be transformed! Men and women would walk into town, sense the presence of the Spirit and fall to their knees in repentance. Church attendance skyrocketed. Prisons were empty because no one committed crimes. Bars went bankrupt because no one wanted to get drunk. The revival was characterized by incredible music and great manifestations of healing. The entire world was affected by this manifestation of God's presence on Earth.

When we read stories about the Welsh revival, our faith begins to rise. We say, "Do it again, Lord!" That's historical faith!

That's why the Bible exhorts us to remember the great works of God in the past. The Feast of the Passover and the observance of the Lord's Supper are both feasts of remembrance, designed by God to help us remember.

It's good to establish memorials to the works of God in our life as well. As we remember what God has done, our faith increases.

2. Saving Faith

Faith and eternal life are inseparably connected. The Presbyterian Church (U.S.A.) catechism says: "Faith in Jesus Christ is a saving grace whereby we receive and rest upon Him alone for salvation, as He is offered to us in the gospel."[2]

From the time the Lord clothed Adam and Eve after the Fall, saving faith became the object of the revealed Word of God. This special act of faith unites a person to Christ (see John 7:38; Acts 16:31). This act of faith justifies a sinner before God (see John 3:16-36; Rom. 3:22,25). A person with this type of faith knows that Jesus is our mediator of all our problems. This type of faith causes a person to trust in and rest in Christ for redemption. A person with this type of faith embraces Jesus as Savior. This type of faith renews our will.

Worship is a response of the will of humankind back to our creator. When we—and the unregenerate also—respond to our creator, this type of worship causes us to take our assigned place in time and creation. We actually begin to fall in with what God is doing on Earth in our generation and align ourselves with it.

This type of faith rests immediately on "thus says the Lord." We hear the Word, the good news, and we respond accordingly. This good news lets us know we can have eternal life. This good news then begins to show us that we can begin to live an abundant life here on Earth. This good news releases us from condemnation and justifies us before God. This type of faith gives us peace with God and begins to sanctify our life (see John 6:37,40; 10:27-28; Rom. 8:1).

3. Temporary Faith

Temporary faith occurs when the Holy Spirit quickens us. We find ourselves in a situation where we lack faith and insight. As we seek the Lord, we receive a quickening from the Spirit. Suddenly we have truth and influence so that we can make the right decision. Temporary faith is a momentary release of faith and revelation from God.

This type of faith must be quickly grounded. I see some individuals receive a quickening touch from God, but then they lose it. In the parable of the sower, Jesus taught that this type of faith can get crowded out by the cares of the world, and the enemy can remove what has been quickened in us (see Matt. 13:3-9,19-22).

This type of faith awakens us but does not keep us awake! Only by developing a lifestyle of worship after we have been quickened can we establish this quickening within our spirit.

4. Supernatural Faith

This is the *gift* of faith. This is a supernatural manifestation of a holy God within our spirit man. It is an instant impartation of faith with regard to a specific need.

I've found that the gift of faith often manifests itself in the

THE GIFT OF FAITH GOES BEYOND NATURAL FAITH AND SAVING FAITH INTO SUPERNATURAL TRUST.

midst of worship. When we worship, our spirit draws into such close fellowship with the Holy Spirit that we begin to know and see as He does.

The gift of faith goes beyond natural faith and saving faith into supernatural trust. When we have supernatural trust, no doubt can shake us from what we have heard.

My wife, Pam, operates in this gift of faith. When Pam begins to pray about an issue that God has put in her heart, she will suddenly know that God has taken care of the issue. That is how the prayer of faith works. This is a supernatural faith. A person who operates in this could be praying for someone who is sick and see him or her as already healed. The actual healing might not manifest itself for another year, but in the heart of the believer who has supernatural faith, *it's done!* I don't usually operate in this level of faith. I usually have to war through the year until the manifestation comes. I call this warfare faith.

5. Warfare Faith

Many of us never overcome because we don't know how to war in faith. What we need to do when we have an issue, a burden or a project that we're praying through is worship until we get a piece of the puzzle.

God speaks to us during worship. From what we hear we war through the next season and gain new ground in our spiritual life. We worship more, and we get more revelation. From this revelation we wage war in the heavenlies until we see the reality manifest itself on Earth.

6. Overcoming Faith

Revelation 12 describes another dimension of faith:

> Then I heard a loud voice saying in heaven, "Now salvation, and strength, and the kingdom of our God, and the power of His Christ have come, for the accuser of our brethren, who accused them before our God day and night, has been cast down. And they overcame him by the blood of the Lamb and by the word of their testimony, and they did not love their lives to the death" (vv. 10-11).

There is an ongoing warfare in the earthly realm. Because the Kingdom has come and is within us, we have the ability to overcome our enemies. When the sound of heaven is imparted into our spirit man, faith arises. This is the sound of triumph. It's the sound of the Blood. It's the sound of authority. It's the sound of redemption. It's the sound of overcoming. Once we appropriate this sound, the victory of the finished work of Christ begins to manifest. We have moved from warfare faith to overcoming faith!

7. Manifested, or Glory, Faith

John 14 tells us, "He who has My commandments and keeps them, it is he who loves Me. And he who loves Me will be loved by My Father, and I will love him and manifest Myself to him" (v. 21).

WE ARE ACTUALLY CLOTHED WITH HEAVEN'S CLOTHING—HIS GLORY.

To manifest is to cause to shine. To manifest is to reveal, appear or come into view. Therefore, God manifests His presence to us, and we feel His presence upon us and in our midst.

I call this glory faith. We are actually clothed with heaven's clothing—His glory. This produces honor, splendor, power, release of wealth, authority, fame, magnificence, dignity and excellence. This is the type of faith that made the individuals of the faith chapter, Hebrews 11, who they were. This is the type of faith we should actually wear in the earthly realm. I believe this is the type of faith that will cover Earth in the latter days.

Having the seven dimensions of faith underscores the biblical thruth that faith *begins* by hearing what God has done in the past. We must take time to remember what God has done for us in the past and observe the memorials given in Scripture of His wonderful deeds. We will then praise Him for the testimonies of others who have trusted Him and seen breakthrough, and we will enter the dimension of historical faith.

Faith is *strengthened* and activated when we hear the Word of God and choose to stand on it. Faith comes by hearing, and hearing by the Word of Christ. Let us fill our mind with the Word! The Bible gives us a foundation for faith. As we allow saving faith to permeate our life, we can be delivered from every aspect of sin and its penalty.

Our faith may be temporarily *quickened* and increased by the Spirit. As we come into new situations and sense the release of faith, we receive temporary faith as a gracious gift of God. When we receive temporary faith, we must be sure to move into a corresponding level of worship. Worship will *establish* in us the faith God has released.

On certain occasions, God *releases* to us the gift of faith as we draw close to Him in worship. Let us thank Him for the gift of faith and give testimony of what He has done. We need to press in to see the full manifestation of His promise.

When we receive revelation from God, we need to engage in warfare against the enemy to see God's purposes established. God calls us to fight the good fight. We can't settle for the status quo or accept passivity. We must stand on God's revelation and *battle* in prayer and allow God to produce warfare faith within us.

As we press through in faith, we overcome. If we stay in the battle until the breakthrough comes, God will produce overcoming faith in us!

The result of overcoming faith is that the glory of God is *manifested* in our midst. God has called us to enter the fullness of His promises. He has called us to live in His glory, clothed in manifested, or glory, faith.

Today who should ask ourselves, *What dimension of faith am I presently walking in?* Then we should ask God what we need to do to enter a new dimension.

Wherever we are, we must keep moving forward! God has called us to the battle to win. A victor's crown awaits us if we overcome. By moving through the seven dimensions of faith, we can overcome the enemy and gain the victory!

A New Dimension of Faith

A shift is a change of place, position or direction. A shift also includes an exchange, or replacement, of one thing for another. A shift is a change of gear so that we can accelerate. A shift can also be an underhanded, or deceitful, scheme. Therefore, in our shift we must recognize that the enemy is plotting to stop it. God is ready for us to shift through our choice to enter into a new dimension of faith. Let us not lean on our understanding but shift into this new dimension of faith!

Here are eight ways to help each of us shift to a new faith level:

1. *Develop His mind-set.* We can't lean on our own under-standing because we will never make the right choice with our limited knowledge. Philippians 2:5-8 makes it clear: "Let this mind be in you which was also in Christ Jesus, who . . . made Himself of no reputation, taking the form of a bondservant. . . . He humbled Himself and became obedient." Romans 12:2

declares, "Do not be conformed to this world, but be transformed by the renewing of your mind, that you may prove what is that good and acceptable and perfect will of God." This simply means we cannot let Satan's scheme shape our thinking to be that of the world. Also, we cannot allow outward appearances to deceive us, causing us to miss what God is doing. We must prove the voice of God and practice in everyday life what God's will from heaven is declaring to us. Romans 8:7 explains: "The carnal mind is enmity against God." We declare that the Lord will put His finger on every area of carnality in our thinking.

2. *Learn to express His heart.* I love to prophesy. We war with our prophecies. Many of us never enter into a new place because we don't know how to war with the word God has given us. However, we forget that prophecy is not just speaking truth. Prophecy is expressing the mind and heart of God. We need to let the Lord deal with our emotions so that they do not interfere with His communicating His heartbeat. We declare that all self-pity and hope deferred are being removed from us. Bitterness and unforgiveness are leaving so that we can express what God is thinking. We will not let inordinate affection cause us to misalign. The heart can have weights or attachments that create shifts. These shifts can prevent us from entering into a new dimension of faith. I declare a free heart over all of us.

3. *Change your atmosphere and speak faith!* Jesus could do very little in Nazareth because the atmosphere was so filled with unbelief. Jesus was the all-powerful God walking the earth, capable of signs and wonders, yet

the atmosphere created a barrier for intervention. Let's break the negative atmospheric presence around us by faith-filled prophetic declarations of victory!

4. *Do exploits! Optimize resources!* Many times what robs our faith is a lack of resources. We can have much vision, but we get frustrated because our vision cannot be accomplished because we have no provision. When we optimize resources, we see what God has presently given us and see how to make that into something else. Only eyes of faith can do this. We see things from a positive standpoint as faith sees! Daniel 11:32 reads, "The people who know their God shall be strong, and carry out great exploits." To do exploits means to take the resources we have and create new resources or bring them into a new level of fullness. This is one of the things that God means when He says to optimize resources.

5. *Know Jehovah Jireh!* We must ask Jehovah Jireh to manifest Himself to us. "Jehovah Jireh" is the first compound name by which Jehovah revealed Himself as the One, the God of revelation, who could open our eyes to see the provision He has for us in the future. This revelation came to Abraham as a result of faith to willingly submit and lay the promise of his future—his only son—on the altar. Jehovah graciously provided a substitute in place of Abraham's son. "Jireh" simply means to see. However, when connected with "Jehovah," the compound name means to see and provide. In other words, when we submit fully, He will show us our provision. That means we will see in advance what we need for our future. God's

provision for us shall be seen on the mount of the Lord. We need to be willing to go up to the place to which He is calling us. That is where we will receive our new, fresh anointing and strategy for provision.

6. *Watch for the suddenlies!* Our faith manifests suddenly at times. However, sometimes we don't expect these suddenlies to occur. If hope deferred and weariness are ruling us, we will miss when God moves on our behalf. If fear is influencing us, we won't understand when God starts breaking through on our behalf. The process that we've been going through is moving toward a suddenly.

7. *Learn the process of going over!* We need to have an "over" mentality. Overtake or be overtaken. Overthrow or be overthrown. Overturn or be overturned. Overcome or be overcome. We need to be sure we are being overseen. We should also know who is overseeing us and whom we oversee. We must remember, faith works in the context of authority.

8. *Develop a Kingdom mentality.* The kingdom of God is within us. We build the Church, but we get keys to the Kingdom. We need to study the Kingdom. Matthew 11:12 declares, "Now the kingdom of heaven suffers violence, and the violent take it by force." The Kingdom advances in victory. This occurs through violent spiritual conflict and warfare. He uses John the Baptist and Elijah to teach us to move forward. Fear not! The Church is God's warring agent. Worship and war! The Kingdom increases. Let us lift up our shield and sharpen our sword because they are both important in God's kingdom conflicts ahead.

THE OPEN DOOR

Revelation is a book that provides deep insight into the nature and tactics of the enemy. In the book of Revelation the apostle John had a supernatural visitation during an extreme time of persecution. In the midst of this persecution, he began to see that the Lord God omnipotent reigns! He seemed to agree with Paul that those who would follow the Lord in their daily life would enter into and be involved in continuing spiritual conflict. As the Lord visited John, He gave him a message concerning the seven key churches of that region. This message also reveals to us God's heart concerning the Church today.

We then find John sharing with us in Revelation 4:1 the following: "After these things I looked, and behold, a door standing open in heaven. And the first voice which I heard was like a

FAITH IN JESUS IS THE ONLY WAY TO ENTER THE KINGDOM OF GOD.

trumpet speaking with me, saying, 'Come up here, and I will show you things which must take place after this.'" The shield of faith is closely related to the concept of a door—the Greek name being thureos, from thura, a square shield that can also be seen as a door. (This shield, used as a weapon, was covered earlier.) A door is an opening for entering or leaving a house, tent or room. The door is used symbolically in the Bible in many ways. We find the Valley of Achor, a place of trouble (see Josh. 7:26), is later promised as "a door of hope" (Hos. 2:15). It will become a reason for God's people to trust Him again. Our trouble can be turned into an entry point into a new place of victory.

Jesus called Himself "the door" (John 10:7,9). Faith in Him is the only way to enter the kingdom of God. God gave to the Gentiles "the door of faith" (Acts 14:27), or an opportunity to know Him as Lord. Jesus stands at the door and knocks (see Rev. 3:20). He calls all people to Himself, but He will not enter without permission. We need to give the Lord permission to take us through new, opportune doors and allow Him to come in and give us the power to go through these doors. Let us open the door of our heart so that we can go through our new door of opportunity.

Paul constantly sought new doors of service! These were open doors for him to go through so that he could minister in the name of Jesus Christ. First Corinthians 16:9 reads, "For a great and effective door has opened to me, and there are many adversaries." There are many doors of opportunity ahead for each one of us. However, the adversaries behind those doors will overtake us unless our door of faith is in place.

Let us lift up our shield, or door, of faith. We do not need to be afraid to go through the opening and into the new places to which the Lord would lead us. Even though many adversaries will be on our path in days ahead, our shield of faith will quench all of their fiery darts. Jeremiah 46:3 (NIV) is encouraging: "Prepare your shields, both large and small, and march out for battle!" Let us go forth with confidence, with our shield lifted high, and our victory will be assured.

Notes

1. Chuck D. Pierce and John Dickson, *The Worship Warrior* (Ventura, CA: Regal Books, 2002), pp. 112-116.
2. *Book of Confession*, part 1 of *The Constitution of the Presbyterian Church (U.S.A.)* (New York: Office of the General Assembly, 1983), item 7.086.

Therefore, having been justified by faith,

we have peace with God through our Lord Jesus

Christ, through whom also we have access by

faith into this grace in which we stand, and

rejoice in hope of the glory of God.

R O M A N S   5 : 1 - 2

SCRIPTURE INDEX

GENERAL INDEX